MW01504912

A REAL BALLBUSTER

Untangling Testicular Cancer Together

Julie B. Hughes

First published by Run to Write 2024

Front cover photo: via Canva.com

All poems were written by the author— Julie B. Hughes

Paperback ISBN: 978-1-7376907-9-5

First edition

Printed in the United States of America

Dear Parents,

This is what I learned when sharing Jeff's diagnosis, procedures, and treatments with my children:

- Conversation worked great over food
- Tell the truth but in bite-size chunks
- Leave space for questions and sadness
- Answer them without anger or avoidance
- Encourage questions— It's okay if you don't know the answer yet.
- Encourage play time (movement), prioritize fun, and consider their routine— stick to it as best as you can.

Our fun Friday ideas:

- Hiking
- Sledding & hot chocolate
- Crafts
- Board games & Card games (we love Clue & Skip-Bo)
- Read aloud with popcorn or a fun snack
- Movie night
- Go out to breakfast
- Drawing & painting
- Making bracelets
- Writing letters
- Baking
- Throwing the football, playing soccer or basketball (movement of any kind)
- Play dates with friends

...ask for and accept help, we need each other, especially during troubles and trials. God Bless.

WHAT PEOPLE ARE SAYING

"Ask for and accept help" might be the most important takeaway from Julie Hughes' new hybrid memoir *A Real Ballbuster, Untangling Testicular Cancer Together*.

This brave and inspirational work never winces or allows the author or readers to close their eyes. Look cancer in the face and tackle it together is what is prescribed. Hughes' book about her husband's and her family's battle with cancer is unsparing in its honesty, but it is also a gentle book that calls on the restorative powers of the natural world and the strength that lies within each of us. Largely prose, this hybrid memoir also features poetry and a shout out, "It's Your Move" to her YouTube channel, at the end of each chapter. A beautiful book helpful to anyone dealing with a crisis or serious illness."

— Nancy Dafoe,
Author of fourteen books, including
Unstuck in Time and Socrates Is Dead Again

"When my children were very small and my husband was going through treatment for testicular cancer, I always said, "It is not something you want to sign up for, but I can tell you this: You can get through it." Julie's story is a testament to 'getting through it.' This book expertly chronicles her family's unexpected medical reality and its uncertain future as they travel together through Jeff's cancer treatments. The upheaval is enormous. The love is forever."

— Katy Dalgleish
Author of *Dear Democracy, You Need us for
Your Success. Sincerely, Public Schools*

"Julie shares her heartfelt emotions and challenges of being thrust into a caregiving role for her husband Jeff's battle with his recurrence of testicular cancer. In addition to raising two children and home responsibilities, Julie shares her journey in a hopeful way and offers encouragement for other caregivers facing a cancer crisis in their lives. Julie emphatically reminds us we are not alone."

— *Bill Tomoff*
Father of 3x childhood cancer survivor,
and passionate cancer support advocate

WHAT PEOPLE ARE SAYING

To Jeff, Brindsley, and Delaney

We made it to the other side wiser, kinder, and stronger. I love you.

"And run with endurance the race that is set before us."

— Hebrews 12:1

Grateful to Creation.

IT'S YOUR MOVE

During Jeff's health crisis, I became very aware of my body's niggles and discomforts. I recognized the importance of movement to relieve stress, calm my nervous system, and boost my spirits. At the end of each chapter, you will find a section titled— **It's Your Move.** A movement will be listed with the link to my YouTube channel. Here you will find a playlist with me demonstrating each movement along with a description.

These are some of my favorite exercises and stretches for getting my body moving, even during hard times. Movement provides renewed energy and optimism. It helps uplift us emotionally and physically.

Try out the movements in my videos. Take what you find helpful and leave the rest. Keeping our bodies active can be an important act of self-care. I hope these exercises provide a positive outlet for you like they did for me.

Take good care,

Julie B.

TABLE OF CONTENTS

What People Are Saying v

It's Your Move ix

Introduction xiii

1. November 2011 1

2. December 2011 3

3. Ten Years Later 7

4. What Does This Mean? 11

5. Emergency Room 15

6. It's Just an Ulcer 19

7. Is This Crazy or What? 25

8. Waiting 33

9. Affirmations 39

10. The 'C' Word 43

11. Joys and Concerns 49

12. Heroes 53

13. Mental Ping Pong 57

14. Color of My Thoughts 61

15. The Playlist 67

16. Bad Luck 69

17. Sweet and Tough 73

18. Happy Valentine's Day 77

19. Wins for the Week 81

20. Manufacture Sunshine™ 85

21. Fun Friday 91

22. Wrestle with Hurt 95

23. Even Though 99

24. Seventeen and The Wig 103

25. Joy in a Basket 107

26. Stressful Pivot 111

27. Expectations of a Caregiver 115

28. Teachable Spirit 119

29. Mud of Life 123

30. Hitting the Wall 127

31. Angels Run 133

32. One More Round 139

33. Hughes Strong 145

34. Run for Jeff 151

35. Miracle Worker 155

36. Tortoise or the Hare? 159

37. God, Turn it Around 163

38. How Is Jeff Doing? 169

Epilogue 171

Affirmations 173

Acknowledgments 175

Resources 179

About the Author 181

INTRODUCTION

I was still on cloud nine. I had just finished The New York City Marathon. For the last four months, Jeff biked alongside me as I trained. Healthy and active, he'd never mentioned feeling sick or off.

I remember when he told me. It was a Saturday morning. I was standing in the hallway between the kitchen and living room. The wooden floor under my feet. Sunshine peeking through the picture window.

"Jules, I have to just come right out and tell you, I found a lump." I scrunched up my face, the word lump made me feel uncomfortable. *A lump? What does he mean?* I didn't understand. *Is this a joke?*

"Well, I was up late watching TV and I felt something uncomfortable, I found a lump in my testicle."

Oh crap. My eyes got wide. My throat tightened and my stomach clenched. I was dumbfounded.

He continued, "I called the doctor. He wants to see me this morning. He already scheduled an ultrasound."

I froze. *A lump, really?* What the heck, could this be cancer?

I asked if he wanted me to go with him to the doctor. He shook his head no. "I'll be fine. I'll let you know when I get back what's going on, it's probably nothing."

I nodded. He gave me a hug and kiss then headed out the door. I remained rooted in the hallway and replayed what he just told me. Could this be cancer? My thoughts paced— *It's got to be something else. He's healthy and strong. What could this be?*

I felt Kole, my black lab, lean up against my leg. I knelt to pet him and then hugged him.

Kole, let's go for a walk, it will keep my mind distracted while we wait for Jeff.

I prayed it was nothing as I hooked the leash onto Kole's collar. Yet something about

Jeff's voice made me concerned. I pulled a hat over my head in hopes it would muffle my internal noise and stepped out into the crisp air. A walk with Kole would help.

CHAPTER 1

NOVEMBER 2011

Jeff returned home with the news I was not prepared for. "The ultrasound was positive—it's testicular cancer."

"What?" I was shocked—*doesn't this show up when you're younger?*

"He cleared a spot for me on Monday for the surgery. He doesn't want to wait."

That's in two days.

"He will need to remove the one testicle. I'm not sure yet if I will need chemotherapy. He also scheduled an appointment at the fertility clinic on Monday morning. His concern is I may not be able to have children naturally after surgery."

I stared at Jeff working hard to gather all the information. It was Saturday. Monday was just around the corner. This didn't allow us time to plan or process. Jeff was a family medicine doctor. His work week was jam-packed with patients. He would need to reschedule them all for the entire week.

How long would recovery be? How much help would he need after? Fertility clinic? I had so many questions but kept them to myself.

Jeff continued, "He wants me to have my sperm frozen in case we can't have children naturally." *What? Children? Oh my gosh.*

I had no time to comprehend. We had to act fast and things were scheduled with no ability to sit down and have a conversation. Looking back, maybe that was for the best. Maybe for me, it was good I didn't have a lot of time to think about it. *I'm great at overthinking.*

Jeff paced our small kitchen.

"I need to tell my parents. I'm going to call them and let them know we will stop over tonight."

I heard the word "we" and winced. I hardly knew his parents— *do I go with him?* This was not easy to navigate and a part of me didn't want to go. We had only been dating for nine months.

I questioned Jeff, "Do you think it would be better if you told your parents alone?"

He was firm in his response. "No, I want you to be there with me."

His blue eyes pleaded with mine. I took a deep breath. *I can do this. I will go with him.*

When we arrived at his parents we made small talk then Jeff got right to business. I recall sitting on the couch next to Jeff in their living room. His parents sitting across from us in comfy recliner chairs listening to this uncomfortable news. I could see their pain and worry. My stomach clenched. My heart raced as he continued. Jeff mentioned he would be having surgery on Monday.

This last sentence brought them to their feet and they rushed over to Jeff. I moved aside so they could sit next to him. Hug him. I pushed back tears. Jeff remained calm and reassured his parents that he would be fine.

"The doctor said I caught it early." His parents nodded. We all sat in silence for a moment. His parents then mentioned Jeff's cousin was also diagnosed with testicular cancer. At the time, I wasn't aware of Jeff's side of the family in terms of medical history. We hadn't gotten to this part of our relationship yet. *Who does?* We were in the early months of dating. Family history wasn't one of our topics for discussion. However, when they mentioned his cousin was doing just fine this brought me hope and I left his parents feeling lighter.

It's Your Move:
Push Up the Clouds
Check out the It's Your Move channel: www.youtube.com/@juliebhughes

CHAPTER 2

DECEMBER 2011

I recall that Monday morning. It was cold with snow on the ground. I ran a few miles with Kole to help clear my mind and calm my nerves. I was thankful to get the day off to be with Jeff. The plan was to head to the fertility clinic and then to the hospital. I was going to stay at the hospital with his parents until he came out of surgery. They suspected he would go home that night.

Kole and I came into the house. Jeff was awake. He came over to cuddle Kole and I hugged him. We needed to head out to the fertility clinic in an hour. My stomach groaned at the thought. I sat on the floor and pet Kole. He relaxed my mind with each pat.

Jeff drove and I didn't recall either of us saying much. The clinic was a short drive and maybe that's why. We stepped into a bustling clinic. Several people sitting in the open waiting room, employees moving in and out of hallways and from behind desks.

I sat in the waiting room while he filled out the paperwork, several sheets stacked on the clipboard. I watched as he moved through each question undisturbed. He made some really tough decisions in minutes. He handed the paperwork in and they brought him into a separate room. I don't remember much of this moment other than sitting alone and wondering how I got here. *Is this really happening?*

I then thought how crazy it was that Jeff had to go into a room by himself to place his sperm in a cup. The idea seemed awkward. *How is he supposed to do that? This office is so busy. This is how it works.* I cringed at my naiveness.

When Jeff came out of the small room I could tell he was uncomfortable. He whispered to me, "That was awful. It would have been nice if the room was in a quieter part of the clinic. It was so noisy, I was afraid someone was going to come in."

My heart hurt. What a strange way to do this. I was relieved we could leave, though our next stop was the hospital. On the drive, he told me he signed a paper that would allow me to have his sperm if something happened to him. I didn't know what to say. What did I say? *I don't remember.*

Marriage and children were something I wasn't thinking about. Yet when Jeff's diagnosis was confirmed our relationship changed in a very short time. We went from talking about sports, running, and where to grab a bite to eat to, *what if the cancer has spread and do we want to get married. Do we want to have children? What if we can't have children?*

The circumstances Jeff and I faced made us stronger, but it also sped up our relationship. *That's what a diagnosis like this will do, change your perspective on life and lean into what's truly important.* I made up my mind. I was all in.

I would be with him as he faced his health challenges. It never crossed my mind to jump ship. I was in the boat with him, rowing when he couldn't. I would be alongside cheering him on just like he did for me all those months training for The New York City Marathon. We were a team and the unexpected gifts we would later receive— marriage and two healthy children.

By the end of Christmas 2011, Jeff was recovering well but it was something we didn't talk much about. It was almost like it never happened. He returned to work one week later and you would never have known what he just went through. Chemotherapy would not be required. I recall the oncologist saying he was cured and it wouldn't come back.

Jeff was diligent with his oncologist appointments for the five years after his diagnosis and no recurrence or spread was detected. In my mind, he was indeed cured. We would move on with this in the rearview mirror. We made it over this obstacle and were grateful to start a family with no difficulty. We had a healthy son, Brindsley on February 11, 2013, and a healthy daughter, Delaney on August 25, 2014.

It was interesting talking to Jeff in 2023 about this first diagnosis. He felt that he was never a true survivor because he only went through surgery. He didn't need chemotherapy and was back to living his life with no real side effects. Even after having one testicle removed his mindset was "It was no big deal." Perhaps this was his way to cope with the loss. *What other option did he have at the time?* There wasn't one.

It's Your Move:

Bridge, Bridge with Single Leg

Check out the It's Your Move channel: www.youtube.com/@juliebhughes

CHAPTER 3

TEN YEARS LATER

It was October 2021. I just achieved my 20-year dream—running The Boston Marathon. I was still glowing weeks later and wasn't paying much attention to Jeff's change in mood. I was on a high and loving life. My focus was still on Boston—meeting Meb Keflezighi, the spectators, Scream Tunnel, and Heartbreak Hill. What an amazing experience we had. I wasn't paying attention to Jeff's complaints of feeling exhausted and off. It wasn't until around Thanksgiving that I started to notice. *Looking back it was around the same time ten years ago when this whole tangle began.*

Jeff was incredibly tired after just walking a few feet and I found him laying on the couch more and more. He was spending less time with me and the kids. He wasn't engaged or present. *What's going on?*

On Thanksgiving day Jeff was extremely lethargic. It took him a while to rally to get out the door. We were headed to the local turkey trot. Brindsley and I were going to run together and Jeff and Delaney would walk.

When I saw Jeff and Delaney come closer to the finish I remember thinking how weary Jeff looked. Delaney picked up the pace into a jog but Jeff wasn't able to pick it up with her like he'd done in the past. After the run, he mentioned he struggled to walk the two miles with Delaney. "I was having a hard time keeping up with her." He chalked it up to being out of shape.

I nodded in agreement. He was out of shape. When was the last time he went for a walk or exercised? It made sense to me. I didn't think much else about his difficulty.

He was speaking with a therapist at the time and they concluded he was depressed. Jeff agreed. His job was stressful and he was struggling with the direction of healthcare. However, without my knowledge, he had been experiencing worrying symptoms - dark stools, dizzy spells at work, and loss of appetite.

He didn't share these things with me but I could tell he was losing weight. I didn't want to say anything, Jeff had always been very sensitive and vigilant when it came to his weight.

I recall after his first diagnosis with cancer, he needed to weigh himself often with his goal to get over 170 pounds which was very hard for him to achieve even when consuming extra calories and strength training. I could tell it frustrated him. Even with the effort and focus he couldn't seem to put on weight. He would hover around 168 to 169 pounds, unable to get to 170 pounds like he wanted.

A few weeks later, I noticed he had lost a lot of weight and he appeared paler. I emphasized his need to get to the doctor. He kind of shrugged it off but luckily his therapist at the time said the same thing. "Get a check-up and then let's go from there."

Looking back, if I had known of his symptoms earlier, dark stool, and dizzy spells at work, I would have been more adamant for him to see a doctor sooner.

We were contemplating the idea that he was depressed but now that we were seeing these physical changes we knew it had to be something else. It was mid-December when he linked up with a doctor and scheduled his new patient appointment. Unfortunately, he wouldn't be seen until mid-January.

Meanwhile, Jeff became more fatigued and withdrew from activities with the kids and me. He would come to the dinner table but would not eat. He was not himself. *This can't be depression* as I watched him becoming paler and thinner. In the back of my mind, I was wondering if it was cancer. I shoved it down not wanting to think about that— not wanting to go there. They said it wouldn't come back so it couldn't be.

* * *

It was the end of December 2021, when Jeff casually walked by me and said "Honey, I've been cancer-free for ten years now." I sat at the kitchen table my pen and notebook in front of me and a cup of coffee. I looked up from my writing and smiled, "Wow, you're right!"

My yellow LIVESTRONG bracelet still going strong, and looked as good as new even though I'd worn it for ten years. I went back to my writing yet this uneasiness came over me. Jeff hadn't been feeling well for the last several weeks. I noticed his appetite had changed and he wasn't feeling like himself. Come to think of it, he appeared to be losing weight.

My mind questioned the cancer-free triumph but I dared not say a word. *Oh my gosh, was his cancer back?* I was mad at myself for having this terrible thought but the more I pieced together the last several months the more anxious I became. I looked up from my notebook and paid deeper attention. I noticed Jeff's pale skin. I noticed his decrease in weight. I noticed his lack of energy. *How could I not say anything?*

I took some deep breaths and then asked, "Jeff, when do you see the doctor?"

He replied, "In a few weeks."

I was relieved he now had a doctor and was on the schedule to be seen. My daily plea of— *please go to the doctor and just get checked out, you haven't been feeling well for a while now*— I could silence. I hoped I was overreacting, maybe it was all because of stress. Yet as January got closer his symptoms got worse.

He found it hard to stay awake on his 55-minute drive home from work. He sat down with us for dinner but only took one bite. He weighed himself— ten pounds lighter than last week. He chalked it up to work-related stress though in my gut I wasn't on board.

When his doctor's appointment finally arrived I was anxious to hear what he would say. What would he recommend? Jeff returned home and filled me in on the plan.

"He ordered blood work and I should get the results in a few days."

"Okay, that's good."

I felt some relief knowing he now had a doctor. I was hopeful we would know soon if there was anything sinister going on. I was praying it wasn't the "C" word.

Jeff seemed in better spirits after his appointment and wondered if he had an ulcer. Yet that night when we sat down for dinner he didn't eat anything and I was concerned. I looked at him from across the table thinking, *gosh he is so pale, something is going on.*

It's Your Move:

Look Up

Check out the It's Your Move channel: www.youtube.com/@juliebhughes

CHAPTER 4

WHAT DOES THIS MEAN?

It was late morning the next day when Jeff called me from work. I was at a coffee shop with my Aunt Colleen. I didn't answer. I figured I would call him back when we were done with our visit but he called again a few minutes later so I answered. This must be urgent.

His voice shook, "Honey, I just looked up my blood work, and isn't good, my iron and hematocrit are really low." Well, that explains why he was so tired and pale. He was extremely anemic. His body wasn't getting enough oxygen-rich blood.

I tried to stay calm, "Okay, so what now?" I gave my aunt a worried look as I took a seat outside the shop. I held my breath for what he would say next.

"I'm going to call the gastrointestinal doctor and see what she says. I'm losing blood somewhere."

Jeff's been to his gastrointestinal doctor before. It was just nine months ago she scheduled him for a colonoscopy and upper endoscopy. He was checked inside and out and besides a few polyps that she removed, he was good and clear. There was nothing sinister in her report.

I nodded, "Okay, let me know if you hear anything. Will you be okay to drive home?"

"Yes, I'll be okay."

I was worried. *He's losing blood and he's still at work.* I was mad. *Isn't there something more we should be doing?*

When I got off the phone my aunt asked if everything was okay. I told her Jeff was losing blood somewhere and wasn't feeling well. She hugged me before we both headed to our cars.

I sat in the driver's seat a bit lost. *What does this mean? Why is he losing blood?* I hope the gastrointestinal doctor can get him in soon.

My phone rang before I had the key in the ignition. It was Jeff.

His voice was clear and calm. "I just spoke with the gastrointestinal doctor she wants to get me in for an upper endoscopy on Monday to examine my upper digestive system. I will need to get a negative COVID-19 test before the procedure but this is good. She thinks it might be an ulcer that is bleeding. She doesn't want me to take any iron pills until after the procedure, it will hinder what she sees on Monday."

I let out a breath I didn't know I was holding. My shoulders and stomach relaxed. Okay, I was glad we were getting some answers. *Let's get you eating foods with lots of iron until you can take the pills.*

"Sounds good, I'm so glad she can get you in soon."

"She would love to get me in sooner but because I need the COVID-19 test, she can't."

"Stupid COVID-19," I muttered under my breath.

Jeff sounded better when we hung up. I felt better that a plan was in place.

As we all sat down for dinner that night I was praying he would eat now that he got some answers but that was wishful thinking. He took one maybe two bites then set down his fork. My heart sank.

Is this really an ulcer? Will an ulcer cause someone to not eat, to lose interest in playing with their children, to have a hard time getting off the couch and getting to work in the morning? He tells me he doesn't feel good and just wants to sleep.

Something more was going on. I wasn't convinced this was a bleeding ulcer. I kept it to myself though and worked hard to keep my mind from going to the dark places. Monday seemed so far away. I was becoming impatient. *Julie, it's just five days away. It's right around the corner.*

Those thoughts allowed me to relax. We would be okay until Monday.

* * *

I could tell Jeff was anxious and unsettled about his blood work results. I remember him repeating, "I'm losing blood, but where?"

Jeff was attempting to diagnose himself. The idea of depression was out the window. Something was going on in his body. He was losing blood and now he could reconcile why he was so tired and dizzy. He could also understand why he was so pale. *Did cancer cross his mind?* He continued to repeat, "It must be an ulcer," but when I asked him later, yes cancer was on his radar.

He then confessed, "Julie, I noticed a few weeks back I was seeing dark tarry stool but I didn't want to believe it. I think I was in denial."

I was shocked. "Wait, what? Jeff, why didn't you tell me? Oh my gosh."

I was not happy he kept this from me but there was no point getting angry at him now. He was sick and I was more angry at myself. I saw him every day becoming more and more fatigued. I saw his appetite and weight change. I saw how pale his feet looked when he walked into the bedroom.

Why didn't I do something? Why wasn't I more aggressive in getting him checked out?

Why didn't I drive him to the hospital? I was beating myself up as I looked at his pale thin face.

My outrageous mind took over—*I'm a terrible wife. Why didn't I do something sooner?*

* * *

I wanted him to take the rest of the week off from work. He was feeling so poor. Now that we knew he was severely anemic, I didn't think it was safe for him to be going to work. He was driving almost an hour each way.

He didn't seem to voice the same concern as me. He didn't seem to be worried about that at all. Jeff figured he could finish the work week and use the weekend to rest before Monday.

I questioned his decision-making.

"What did the doctor say? Didn't he think you should stay home until we know what's going on?"

"He didn't say anything," his voice indifferent.

I'm not sure what he was thinking. I told him I didn't want him to keep working but he said he would be fine. He would wait until Monday to see what the gastrointestinal doctor would tell him. This was his way, keep going even when he felt so poor.

He'd been struggling like this for about two months now. Why did I think he would change in the last three days of hearing this news? I thought he would. I didn't think it was a good idea. But apparently, I was the only one. His primary doctor was concerned about the low blood and how anemic he was but from what I remember nothing was said. Why was there no urgency in this matter?

I thought it was odd that there wasn't more happening to help my husband. Here it was Wednesday and we needed to wait until Monday to find out where he was losing blood. I was angry.

I didn't want to believe this could be cancer yet it crossed my mind after learning he was extremely anemic. I pushed the thought away each time it came up and I didn't say it to Jeff. I was praying he would make it through the week.

It's Your Move:
Pump Water (*an invitation to grab a tall glass of water*)
Check out the It's Your Move channel: www.youtube.com/@juliebhughes

CHAPTER 5

EMERGENCY ROOM

Jeff woke up Friday morning to get ready for work and felt awful. He was clammy and nauseous.

I found him leaning over the bathroom sink, "I feel so dizzy."

I placed my hand on his shoulder, "I think you better stay home today Jeff, there is no way I want you driving almost an hour to work when you're feeling dizzy."

He looked terrible and needed to see someone. He was attempting to get ready for work.

I looked him in the eyes, "We need to get you to the emergency room."

He replied, "No I'll be okay, help me to the couch so I can rest a bit, maybe I'll feel better."

He took his hands off the bathroom counter and almost dropped to the floor. "I think I'm going to pass out." We stood there for a moment together before he was ready to move again.

I had no idea how we managed to stay standing but we did. I rushed him down the hallway to the couch to lie down. My heart raced, grateful we made it.

Jeff closed his eyes, "I'm not feeling well at all. I feel worse than yesterday."

I replied in a firm voice, "You need to stay home and I'm going to take you to the hospital. I'm going to call your boss and tell her you won't be in."

He nodded, "Let me rest, you can take the kids to school then we can go."

"Okay, I'm going to drop the kids off then I'll come back and take you to the hospital." I was not backing down. He needed to be seen.

I called his supervisor and left her a message that Jeff would not be coming to work because he would be in the hospital. I left with the kids praying he would be alright until I got back. My mind raced— I hoped I could get him to the car without him passing out on me. *Do I call an ambulance instead? He is so pale and thin.*

I was scared.

My stomach clenched and my mind raced with worry as I pulled out of our driveway.

Yet as I drove Brindsley and Delaney to school their laughter and singing carried me. My fear took a backseat and my focus shifted to them. I joined in and my stomach and shoulders relaxed.

I pulled into the school parking lot circle to drop them off at the curb, the standard procedure. I gave Brindsley and Delaney hugs and kisses before they headed out of the car. I told them I would pick them up after school. They waved as I drove off.

My worries returned as I sat in the empty car and headed back to the house. I missed my children's voices. I prayed Jeff was okay for me to drive him to the hospital. I prayed this was nothing serious yet I had a feeling I was wrong.

I pulled into the driveway and rushed inside. Jeff was right where I left him. "You ready to go?"

"Yes, I might just need some help."

I grabbed his arm and we walked together to the car. I was relieved he was able to walk on his own. As we drove to the hospital we didn't talk much. I recall the drive— uneasy and quiet. Jeff mentioned he thought one visitor was allowed into the emergency room and that gave me comfort. I wanted to see if Monday's procedure could be pushed up to today. I was concerned about his blood work. He was losing blood for goodness' sake.

When we arrived at the Emergency Room we didn't wait long. I was surprised and grateful. We both were taken back to a room and a nurse came in shortly after. Jeff shared his story and the blood work results from the beginning of the week. He told her his appointment with the gastrointestinal doctor was on Monday for an upper endoscopy to rule out an ulcer.

She looked Jeff over and checked his vitals. He was placed on an IV for hydration. She turned to her computer and began typing away. She put in orders for more blood work and a CT scan.

Jeff was more relaxed and in good spirits as we waited for the next clinician to come in and take his blood. I was too.

Once that was complete they rolled him out of the room for the CT scan. I sat in the small room and waited. I texted my mom just in case I would need her to help pick up the kids. I was hoping we would get out in time but wanted a backup plan in case.

Jeff wasn't gone long and we waited together until the nurse came in with the results from his blood work and CT scan. She confirmed, "Yes, you're severely anemic and losing blood, by the looks of your CT scan we think it might be from an ulcer. Your stomach is very inflamed and the duodenum is thickened." (*The duodenum is the first part of the small intestine. It is located between the stomach and the middle part of the small intestine.*)

Jeff's face didn't seem convinced though he nodded and was polite. When he heard thickened duodenum he knew his cancer was back but didn't say anything. He wasn't capable of making these decisions in the shape he was in or maybe he was still holding onto hope that it was indeed an ulcer. Either way, I wasn't aware of his thinking and I didn't poke for his thoughts on the visit. It wasn't the time or place.

She encouraged him to eat iron-rich foods until Monday. I was hoping for something more but they discharged him and believed he would be fine until then. I was praying that he wouldn't pass out or get worse over the weekend.

His fatigue and lack of appetite continued and my worry too. He looked so sick and Monday couldn't' come soon enough. I didn't say anything to Jeff but I had a feeling we were dealing with something bigger than an ulcer. Cancer was now on my mind and I couldn't shake the thought.

Unbeknownst to me Jeff was thinking the same thing. We didn't share our thoughts. I stayed silent. I was working hard to ignore the deep feeling in my bones— this was not an ulcer.

We were both uneasy after Friday's episode. I was becoming impatient while we waited for Monday's upper endoscopy. I encouraged Jeff to stay hydrated and to rest. I was praying he would make it to Monday.

It's Your Move:

Child's Pose

Check out the It's Your Move channel: www.youtube.com/@juliebhughes

CHAPTER 6

IT'S JUST AN ULCER

Monday finally came. I dropped Jeff off for his procedure around 11 a.m. They told me it shouldn't be long, maybe an hour. They would call me when it was time to pull up to the building to pick him up. They would walk him out to the car. They didn't want me to come inside. Jeff grabbed his mask and headed into the clinic.

I passed the time by writing and reading in the car. At around 12:30 p.m., I started to become concerned and impatient. I decided I needed to walk around so I drove over to Costco and wandered inside the store to keep my mind off the worst-case scenario. I didn't know what to do with myself randomly staring at boxes and bags of items. I had no direction or purpose for why I was in there other than to distract my worried mind. I felt lost until I saw the restroom sign in big bold letters.

I headed in that direction and stepped inside. *Okay, I did have a purpose for being here. I'll use the bathroom.* Who knew how much longer Jeff would be, plus with the two cups of coffee I had at breakfast I figured I better go now. After I used the restroom I headed out to my car. As I was making my way across the parking lot my phone rang. I didn't recognize the number—*this must be the nurse.* I answered and the nurse announced that Jeff's procedure was done.

I responded, "Oh good, I'll head right over." Then he continued, "The doctor wants to talk to you both, I'll come out and get you. Please have a mask on."

My stomach dropped. I felt sick. *Why would the doctor need me to come in if it's just an ulcer? This can't be good.* I took deep breaths to relax and prayed that my gut was wrong. I parked the car, put on my mask, and was greeted at the front entrance. The nurse brought me into a space closed off by curtains where Jeff was resting in bed.

He was hooked up to an IV drip, his eyes still closed. He looked sick. I walked up to his bedside and grabbed his hand. His eyes began to open and I smiled at him.

He gave me a faint smile back. I was glad he was happy to see me. I told him the doctor wanted to talk to us both. His smile then disappeared. I think he was thinking the same thing—*why does my wife need to be here if it's just an ulcer?*

I'm sure you have now guessed— Jeff was indeed losing blood but not because of an ulcer.

I held Jeff's hand in silence as we waited for the doctor. I was thinking the worst when she walked in and greeted us. "I want to show you what I found." She held up several small square images on one sheet of paper. The pictures were of Jeff's duodenum, the first part of the small intestine. It was very very red and she pointed to a spot on the image that was concerning.

She spoke from under her mask, "This isn't an ulcer but I'm not sure what it is so we are sending a biopsy off immediately. I'm asking for rush results. We hope to know very soon."

UGH. My stomach clenched and my heart began to race. *Breath Julie breath I repeated to myself. Stay calm.* My chest tightened and I did my best to hold off the tears. I was glad at that moment for the mask. It covered my expression well. I stood there in silence.

Jeff spoke up "Do you think this is adenocarcinoma?"

She responded, "Maybe, I just don't know, let's not get ahead of ourselves. Let's wait until we get the results."

I then repeated what Jeff asked, "Do you think this is cancer?"

She looked at me with worried eyes, "I don't know yet."

I squeezed Jeff's hand. He looked at me, "Are you okay?" I nodded working hard to keep my composure. The doctor thanked me for coming in and would be in touch as soon as she knew something. She tried her best to reassure me before she left. Her nurse came in and asked me to head back out to the car. They would wheel Jeff out when he was dressed and ready.

I kissed Jeff on the cheek. My self-control held on until I opened the exit door. I stepped out into the cool air and so did my tears. I rushed to the car. My heart raced. My vision blurred. The gastrointestinal doctor's words, "This is concerning, rush biopsy, this isn't an ulcer," replayed in my mind.

My breath moved faster and faster. *Am I dreaming?* My muscles started to shake. I had to get it together. I needed to drive us home. I closed my eyes— and focused hard on my breathing. I needed to slow my breathing down. I placed my hand on my heart. *Julie, you can do this, just focus on your breath. God is with you.*

I managed to slow my breathing and shifted my focus to what I could control. My thoughts about this circumstance and my response. I took a few deep breaths and this soothed my muscles.

Okay, let's wait to see what the biopsy shows, until then focus on getting Jeff foods rich in iron and pray.

I opened my eyes to see Jeff being wheeled out to the car. I prayed I could keep it together on the drive home. The plan before this news was to stop for lunch since he was instructed to not eat anything in the morning before the procedure. However, he didn't want to eat, "Let's just get home."

I nodded. I wasn't in the mood for food either. I started the car and Jeff got on his phone. He started texting some of his colleagues for help and advice. We coped in different ways. We didn't have much information other than he was losing blood and he was already coming up with what it could be. What the plan would be if it's this or if it's that? I had to just keep my mouth shut, breathe, pray, and drive.

He is handling it in his own way. It's not my way and that's okay.

He got home and went right to the computer looking up signs and symptoms of duodenal cancer and on and on. I was mad. "Jeff please don't get ahead of yourself. Let's stay level-headed and patient until we know what this is. It could be something other than cancer."

I said those words wanting to believe them. I didn't though. I had already made up my mind that this was cancer and we just needed to know what kind. Jeff was thinking the same. Within 15 minutes of arriving home, he was on the phone with a surgeon discussing what he had learned so far. A self-diagnosis of duodenal cancer was on his mind and he wanted to know the surgical treatment. I couldn't take it. I was angry that he was going down this rabbit hole when we didn't know for certain what we were dealing with. I left the room and tried to stay calm but I had so many emotions—anger, sadness, fear, anxiety.

GRR…weren't we just acknowledging ten years of being cancer-free—didn't the doctor say this would never come back, that he was cured? I was furious. What was I supposed to tell Brindsley and Delaney? *This is awful.*

As Jeff talked in the other room I left to pick up the kids from school. I didn't want to listen to his conversation and needed some space. I wanted to be alone. Once I got in the car my mind was racing with the events of today. I wanted to talk to someone. I needed to process this out loud. I decided to vox my friend. I knew she would be at work and unable to answer the phone so Voxer was the next best thing. It was a walkie-talkie app on my phone. I could leave a message and she would be able to listen when it was convenient for her. She could then vox me back at her convenience. I grabbed my phone and hit the button. As I drove out of the driveway, I told her everything. It felt good to speak it aloud and I needed to get it out of my mind before I picked up the kids.

I shared what was going on to help myself process the events from today. I asked her for prayers and I would be in touch as soon as I knew more. I didn't want to tell anyone else yet. I wanted to know more. I felt calmer as I parked the car and walked into the school to wait for the kids. Yet as I stood there my mind raced with questions—

*What are we going to do? Is he going to work tomorrow? Should he still be working? Is he going to need surgery or chemotherapy or both? I hope this isn't cancer...*just then my eyes met my children's. I forced a smile and hugged them tight. I was so happy to see them but dreaded what I may have to tell them when the time came.

We all jumped in the car and the kids talked the entire way home about their day. I was happy for the diversion. Once we got home I prayed Jeff was off the phone and wouldn't mention anything in front of the kids. I wanted to know what we were up against and the plan before we told them. Jeff agreed. We needed to be patient and I pleaded with Jeff to stop looking stuff up until we heard from the gastrointestinal doctor.

We sat down for dinner that night but Jeff didn't eat. He looked down at his food but couldn't get himself to take a bite. I tried to keep a poker face, yet my worry and concern were tough to hide. Brindsley and Delaney could tell something was wrong. Jeff looked up at them and knew he needed to tell them why he was so tired and didn't have much energy.

He cleared his throat and shared with the kids that he was anemic, "I don't have enough healthy red blood cells and that's why I've been so tired." He mentioned he was having more tests to figure out why. Brindsley and Delaney seemed to be satisfied with that explanation and didn't ask anything more. I chimed in with, "This is why Dad hasn't had the energy to play with you, he's not feeling well but we hope to know more soon so he can." I smiled to reassure them.

It's Your Move:
Flip a Pancake— Palm Up, Palm Down
Check out the It's Your Move channel: www.youtube.com/@juliebhughes

Chapter 7

IS THIS CRAZY OR WHAT?

Pain can come
out of nowhere
No fall
No injury
I'm not even sick
Yet my left ankle is throbbing
And the output is to limp

What was the input?
What turned up the alarm
I didn't turn funny
I didn't trip
My nutrition is great
Is it my mind playing tricks?

Quick-
get me an ice pack
And some wine (not really I don't drink wine)
I'll lie down
Retrace my day
Why does my ankle
have so much to say?

Is it really about this afternoon?
What the doctor said…
This is concerning, a biopsy will be sent
My entire body felt cold

A Real Ballbuster

I froze—
could cancer be taking hold?

I grabbed my husband's hand
as he sat in the bed,
pale and weak
I kissed his cheek

My mind raced with all
sorts of terrible thoughts
Could that be the reason
my left ankle feels like
it's in knots?

I'll take some deep breaths
This doesn't mean death
My brain has it wrong
My ankle is fine and strong

I will not freak out
I know what this pain is about
I will move my ankle as
I read to my son
I will get a good night's sleep
an optimistic attitude I will keep

Though my nerves are on high alert
I have some ways to turn it down
What I say
and believe about my
ankle is more important now—

This discomfort is temporary
I'm physically fine
My nervous system is
looking out for me
during this time.

Pain is so weird
So strange at times
I woke up the next day
sore but fine—a run will
do me some good to
clear my mind.
Movement I love to
decrease the protection
and give my body evidence
that we are moving in the right
direction.

—Thank you brain but I got this

That night as I was making the kid's lunches for school my right ankle started throbbing. I was standing in front of the kitchen counter chopping veggies and fruit. I didn't think much of it until I turned to walk toward the refrigerator to put the lunches away. I took two steps, gasped in pain, and stopped. What the heck? I was surprised by the discomfort. I couldn't put weight on my right foot and when I did I got tremendous pain in the front of my ankle and the bottom of my foot.

I limped to the refrigerator, placed the kid's lunches inside then opened the freezer. Maybe an ice pack would help as my mind searched for what I did wrong. This pain came without any warning. I couldn't remember twisting it on my run or any injury. I'd been fine all day. What had changed? Everything!

Oh, that's right, Jeff has some unusual tumor growing in his duodenum. I'm angry, scared, sad, anxious, and wondering how I'll tell Brindsley and Delaney if this is cancer.

Okay, of course, I had pain—these emotions were flooding my nervous system and the harm alarm was going off. I didn't do anything to injure my ankle however that wasn't required to feel pain. I just found out that my husband most likely had cancer, a huge threat, and my nervous system was aware and processing it all. I couldn't explain why the output was ankle pain but it was. The weirdest part— I had identical discomfort and symptoms in 2011.

It was a similar occurrence, the pain began without an injury that I was aware of. It just happened out of the blue. I walked into the grocery store and a few minutes later I found myself limping through each aisle. What happened? I began to panic. *Will I be able to make it up to the register? Will I be able to walk to my car?*

I coached myself as I grabbed one more item before making my way up to the cashier. I was embarrassed by my limp and tried to hide the pain as I waited in line. I hobbled out happy to find my car not parked as far as normal. I couldn't believe how much pain I was in. *Do I have plantar fasciitis? I'm not going to be able to run tomorrow if this keeps up.*

I was training for The New York City Marathon and was freaking out about missing any time in my training. I needed to run. I was not going to let this pain get the best of me. I was just turning a corner in my pain recovery and now this? I was so frustrated because I couldn't figure out what I did wrong. *Is it from running? Is it from all the strengthening I'm doing?*

What else was going on at the time? This was one question I didn't bother to ask in my angst. However, a lot was going on and I didn't consider the other factors that can contribute to pain.

I wasn't happy with my job. I was taking courses at night to consider starting a Physical Therapy practice. Jeff was opening a new building for his practice and there was talk that I would go over there. My view was nothing was happening. I wasn't talking to my mom as she was going through a divorce with my dad. *Pain is weird.* Yet it had something to tell me. I had more to learn.

Oddly, this memory reassured me. *This discomfort is temporary.* Don't forget what you know about pain, Julie. I reached in for the ice pack and hobbled to Brindsley's bedroom. It was my turn to put him to bed. I was happy I would be able to get off my feet and ice while I read to him. Brindsley was already reading to himself when I came in limping.

He looked up, "What happened, Mom."

"Oh, I'm having some discomfort in my ankle. I'll be okay."

I sat at the edge of his bed to see if I could move my ankle up and down but was met with tremendous pushback. "Ouch," I whispered. I closed my eyes and took some deep breaths. It hurt to move in any direction. I found it comical that just 30 minutes ago I was walking around with no problem now I could hardly move. *Is this crazy or what?*

I placed the ice pack on the front of my ankle and began to read to Brindsley. I don't recall what book we were reading, I wish I did, but I remember laughing and smiling. My ankle pain softened. I took off the ice and was now able to move it a little bit up and down, better than before.

I continued to read as I moved my ankle in the directions I could tolerate. *The movement will help.* The reading and the company were a great distraction from the events that took place earlier. *Laughter will help. What I say to myself matters—this is temporary, see you can move your ankle with less discomfort. This pain is not permanent.*

When I left Brindsley's room my limp was not as severe. I felt some peace and comfort knowing that my ankle wasn't injured. *I will keep moving it and pay attention to what I say to myself. I will get a good night's sleep.* I set my alarm to get up for a run. I would see how I felt in the morning. I knew movement was beneficial and if I could put weight on my ankle without limping then I would run.

When I woke up the next morning I forgot for a moment about my ankle until the ache reminded me. I was surprised I could walk to the bathroom without a limp. I was able to push off without wincing. It was sore but I could place all my weight on my foot without a problem. I was safe. This gave me the green light that I could run.

Even though the front of my ankle was very sore and my range of motion was not restored I knew a run would help. Running makes me happy and my way to process life's challenges and troubles. *Running is rehab.*

I got dressed and headed out the door, thrilled to see the stars glittered overhead. The moon reflected a path for me on the road. I was not alone. This would benefit my body and mind.

I wasn't the only one who would experience physical pain during this challenge. My daughter Delaney, 7 years old at the time, was having moments of limping and complaining of her entire right leg hurting. I recall this occurring a month into Jeff's chemotherapy treatments.

"It hurts so bad Mom," I recall her lying in bed groaning and rolling around grabbing her leg. I felt awful.

I would ask her if she fell or remembers doing anything to hurt herself and she said no. It just came on.

I recall one afternoon picking her up from school for an orthodontist appointment. I was waiting in the school entryway for her to come meet me. She turned the corner limping. She was on her right tippy toes unable to place weight on her right foot. *What happened?*

"Hi Delaney, is your foot bothering you?"

She looked down at her leg, "Yes, it hurts to put weight on my foot."

"Did you have a fall?"

"No, it just started bothering me a while ago."

I didn't press further and walked with her to the car trying to hide my concern. Did the teacher notice? Why didn't they call me? Why would she be limping if she didn't injure her right leg?

Oh, how easy I forget— **pain doesn't always mean injury.**

I stood next to her to see if she needed help getting in the car but she did fine. I was relieved. I turned on the music in hopes a song would come on we could sing to. Maybe this would cheer her up as we headed towards the orthodontist ten minutes away.

We sang the entire drive and Delaney was all smiles. When we reached our destination I was curious if she would still be limping once she got out of the car. Nope.

She hopped out, grabbed my hand, and walked into the Orthodontist with no problem.

I didn't say a word.

Coincidentally, Delaney experienced recurrent knee and ankle pain throughout Jeff's cancer treatment. The same spontaneous aching and limping would arise unexpectedly - she'd be active and carefree one minute, then limping to me hours later complaining of her discomfort. Despite the vagueness of the symptoms, this pattern repeated itself several times during those challenging months.

The location of her pain would vary - sometimes the left leg, sometimes the right. It would start in her foot, and then travel to her knee or thigh. To help her, I would massage her leg, play games as a distraction, sing songs, and reassure her that Daddy would be okay. I promised I would take good care of her and always be there.

This was hard. It was difficult to see my daughter carrying this burden of worry and anxiety. I found it interesting that her pain showed up very similar to mine. I didn't want to assume though— I could be wrong so I examined her knee. I made sure she had a full range of motion both active and passive. I performed some other tests I learned in physical therapy school to make sure I wasn't missing anything. Everything checked out. Nothing stood out to me and none of the tests recreated her symptoms. I was still worried.

I called my good friend Jeanne who was a physical therapist to get some advice. I shared with her what was going on and the tests I performed to see if she had any other ideas. I was happy I could talk about this with her with no judgment. She was thinking the same— "Julie, you're in the middle of a crisis and this is how your daughter's body is letting her know."

I was grateful to Jeanne, for her wisdom and reassurance. Looking back, I needed this kind of support. I was blessed I had a friend to help me. I had a friend I could call.

It's Your Move:
Ankle/Foot Alphabet
Check out the It's Your Move channel: www.youtube.com/@juliebhughes

CHAPTER 8

WAITING

The waiting is hard—
my imagination runs
to the dark places
Fear on my right
Trouble on my left
Would you pray for me?

The next few days dragged on as we waited to hear the biopsy results. Jeff continued to go to work but his anxiety was up and he wasn't eating. *Why won't he take a few days off?* I was confused by his decision to keep working.

I prayed we would hear from the doctor soon. I went for my run and brought my phone in case Jeff needed to call me. Of course, it was zero degrees and my phone died five minutes into the run. *Oh well, I'll get in touch with him when I'm done.* I focused on the snow covered fields, the distant sounds of geese, and my breath. I was surprised how calm my mind was. I was grateful I chose to run. It was one way to relieve my stress and worry.

As soon as I got home, I plugged my dead phone into the charger. After kicking off my sneakers, I checked the screen - it was at just 1% battery left. I knew it would take some time before any new messages came through while it was charging.

I peeled off my gloves and hat, I went back to check my phone and a notification showed up. Jeff called while I was running and left me a message to call him back. With my phone plugged in I took a seat and dialed his number. I was grateful he answered.

My heart sank when he said, "It's cancer but they don't know what kind. They think maybe it's lymphoma but not 100%. She said it's in a weird spot."

The cancer was found in his duodenum which was odd and unusual if it was seminoma.

He mentioned she was going to have several doctors check the biopsy to make sure they got it right. It was important to know which type of cancer before moving forward with treatment. In the meantime, she made a referral to Dr. Duffy, an oncologist. His office would call Jeff to set up an appointment. I prayed they could get him in this week.

"I can't believe this." I held back tears. Jeff sounded calm on the other end, "I know, but this explains why I've been feeling so crappy."

"I love you, please let me know if you hear anything from Dr. Duffy's office."

"I love you too, Jules," and we hung up.

I stayed in the chair for a moment trying to process what he just said. *Why is he still working? I don't understand why no one tells him to rest, his iron is so low. He has cancer!*

My stomach clenched. My chest tightened. *He has cancer. How will I tell the kids?* I prayed we would get into the oncologist by the end of the week. I prayed the Lord would give me the words when it was time to tell the children.

Jeff called me 30 minutes later. "Honey, they can get me in today at 1:15 p.m. with Dr. Duffy. This is great. Can you meet me there?"

"Yes, of course, I'll get ready and head out soon."

"Okay, I'm going to wrap things up here at work and leave in ten minutes so I can get there in time."

We hung up. I closed my eyes.

Thank you, Lord, for answering my prayer.

Jeff was checking in when I arrived at the Hematology-Oncology Associates of CNY center. I was thankful I remembered a mask as they were still mandatory at healthcare facilities. I was so happy to see him. He arrived safe. He had pages of paperwork to fill out, stacked on a clipboard. I could tell he was tired and frustrated with it all. He filled out a couple of lines, then lifted his pen and stopped. He took a long exhale. I offered to help but he said, "No, I'll just take my time."

We were called into a small office on the first level to go over his paperwork and learn more about their clinic...insurance, payments, patient portal, services offered, etc. Once we finished the meeting we were sent upstairs to wait for the nurse and Dr. Duffy. We sat next to each other in silence. I looked around at all the people waiting. There were so many people.

I glanced at my watch and realized I wasn't going to be back in time to pick up the kids from school. I called the school hoping I wasn't too late to switch them to the bus. The front office was great on the phone and had no trouble switching them. I called my mom to see if she could be at our house to get them off the bus. I had no idea how long we were going to be here and I didn't want to rush.

I was relieved my mom answered and was free to help us with such short notice. It was once I hung up that the nurse called out Jeff's name. She brought him over to record his weight and height. He knew he lost weight but had no idea how much. The scale read 159 pounds—to put this into perspective Jeff was over six feet tall.

The nurse recorded the numbers and then brought us back to a room where we would see the doctor. We didn't wait long when a registered nurse came in, followed by Dr. Duffy. They both were very gentle and kind with their approach and that gave me peace. Dr. Duffy went right to the optimistic viewpoint which I needed, "This is very treatable with chemotherapy but I would like to have an exact diagnosis before moving forward with a treatment plan."

He looked at Jeff with concerned eyes, "How are you working? We need to get your iron levels up right away. You probably feel really bad. I'm going to order an iron infusion, this will at least start helping you feel better."

Jeff and I were both in agreement and very happy to hear about the infusion. He ordered a PET scan to see if the cancer had spread to other areas of his body, an iron infusion, and blood work. Jeff's hematocrit was severely low. Dr. Duffy wanted to improve his levels before any treatment but he also wanted to check if it was dropping from when it was last checked.

He recommended Jeff begin an iron pill as we waited for the iron infusion date. Dr. Duffy was confident that once he had the iron infusion his fatigue would improve. He told him to get things in order so he could take time off from work and focus on the tests and procedures he would need before chemotherapy. Dr. Duffy also mentioned we get a second opinion and gave us some recommendations. I was surprised by this yet respected him even more. He cared and was doing the right thing. I felt like he was treating us how he would a brother or family member. I could tell on our first visit, that we were in good hands. I was grateful the gastrointestinal doctor referred us to him.

Thankfully when Jeff checked his blood work on the patient portal the next day, it was the same. I took that as a great sign. Jeff was disappointed it wasn't higher. I had no idea why he would think that he just started the iron pill yesterday.

I was grateful, "At least it isn't lower, it's the same so you're not losing blood fast."

He was not in a good place and every thought was bringing him further down into despair. It was hard to watch but could I blame him? He felt awful and his cancer was back.

He was acting like he was dying. I was frustrated. We didn't even know what we were up against. Jeff was already thinking it wasn't treatable and he wasn't going to get better. GRR. This went on until Friday. I realized I needed support. I called the Pastor at the church that we just started attending. I was nervous and questioned the call. *Should I ask him? Is this okay even though we just started attending service a few months ago?*

I was grateful I pushed my fear aside and called Pastor Kim. I asked if he could come over and pray with Jeff. "His thoughts are not good at all and he is acting like he is dying. I'm trying to stay supportive but I'm feeling frustration in me."

Pastor Kim was kind and gentle with his response. "I can come on Saturday at 4 p.m."

I thanked him. I felt at peace. I felt lighter. This heaviness I didn't know I was carrying was less with a simple phone call for help.

I was trying to convince myself that Jeff would be okay once we had more information and could start treatment. Jeff expressed the opposite view, "I keep thinking I'm not going to get better. I feel so poor." While I wanted to believe starting treatment would help him recover, Jeff was voicing hopelessness about his condition. My heart ached.

Later that day we got a call to schedule his iron infusion. We were hoping they could fit him in for Monday but didn't have any openings until Friday— another week we would need to wait. I prayed hard that some way an opening would appear in their schedule and Jeff would be able to get in sooner. I prayed for God to give Jeff comfort and strength to endure the road ahead. I prayed Jeff would turn his face towards God rather than turn away. I prayed the same for myself.

It's Your Move:
Open Heart with Rotation
Check out the It's Your Move channel: www.youtube.com/@juliebhughes

CHAPTER 9

AFFIRMATIONS

It was just last week Delaney came home from school and started talking about cancer and how people die from it. My heart sank. Where did she hear this from? I told her there were many types of cancer and many were treatable, not everyone dies from cancer. She was happy with that response and went off to play. I was terrified. *Will Jeff's cancer be treatable?* I was not looking forward to having this conversation with them. *How long can I wait to tell them?*

When Pastor Kim arrived on Saturday I was nervous. I didn't know what to tell the children. I didn't want them to hear the word cancer yet. I was stressed that it may slip out when he was praying over Jeff so I decided I would have the children play in our bedroom. It was located in the back of the house. I would shut the door. The one time I wished we had a two-story home.

I grabbed his hand and held it tight. "Jeff, the Pastor is coming at 4 p.m., he will pray for you."

"What about the kids," his voice concerned.

"I'll take them to the back room and we can play cards or something. It will be fine. It's okay for them to know the Pastor is here to pray with you. That's all they need to know for now."

He nodded and then laid back down on the couch. I decided to tidy up the place before he came. I noticed this was my way to cope and distract my mind—clean. I mopped the floors and cleaned the stove. I couldn't recall the last time I mopped the kitchen floor. It felt good to see clean, shiny floors when I was finished. The house smelled fresh. I felt a sense of accomplishment.

Jeff was still on the couch resting until the Pastor pulled into the driveway. I grabbed the kids and asked them to stay in the back part of the house so the Pastor could talk with Dad. They were fine with it and didn't ask questions. They were curious though and I told them they could come out to see Pastor Kim and say hi in a bit.

I was happy to see Pastor Kim. He pulled up a chair next to Jeff and they talked. I could see Jeff's body relax as he sat there on the couch sharing what he was facing. I went back and forth between Jeff and the kids pacing the hallway. I didn't know what to do with myself. Do I sit there with Jeff? Do I give him some privacy with the Pastor? I voted for the latter and sat with the kids for a while. My mind was not quiet. It was full of questions, fears, worries, and *how am I going to tell my children?*

That seemed to be the loudest of all. It was the question I didn't know how to answer. It was the question that was keeping me up at night.

Please Lord give me wisdom and words when the time comes. Who else could I ask but the Lord? It was the best I could do for now— pray and ask for wisdom.

The kids were playing with Legos so I went back out to check on Jeff. He was lying on the couch and the Pastor was praying over him. I watched from the hallway. I didn't want to intrude or disturb their time. Pastor Kim placed his hands on the right side of Jeff's stomach and prayed for healing.

He was in great spirits when Pastor Kim left and he said he felt better. Jeff mentioned, "A lot of this is in my mind, the things I'm saying to myself, I know it." I shook my head. I didn't say it out loud but I could certainly relate. His sickness was real but what we think and say adds to our suffering, adds to our pain.

At some point we would need to accept this was what was happening. There was nothing we could do to change Jeff's situation. However, what we think, believe, and say to ourselves matters in any circumstance.

I don't like what is happening, yet I can handle it or I don't like what is happening but I have a choice of how I will show up for my family. Two affirmations I was writing down in my journal and saying to myself to shift my mind. I could choose faith or fear. I could choose courage over comfort.

I'm beginning to believe he will be okay. I'm beginning to believe he will have the strength to make it through. Does Jeff believe these things? I wonder.

It's Your Move:

Chair Squats or Standing Squats

Check out the It's Your Move channel: www.youtube.com/@juliebhughes

CHAPTER 10

THE 'C' WORD

I was sitting on the couch reading when Jeff's phone rang. The kids were at the other end of the house playing.

Jeff grabbed his phone, "It's Dr. Duffy, he must have the biopsy results."

He paced the kitchen in silence while I sat on the couch attempting to read. My focus was distracted. I heard a lot of "Hmmm." "I know." "Okay." I closed my book hoping to catch some of their conversation. Jeff then came into the living room and sat down next to me. He looked at me, placed his hand over the receiver, and whispered, "It's testicular cancer, it came back." I grabbed his hand while he continued his conversation with Dr. Duffy.

We were prepared for this but I felt sick. I thought this never would come back.

Jeff hung up the phone. He looked at me. "The doctor said it's stage three seminoma. It's from my testicular cancer ten years ago. He said I would need a lot of chemotherapy and it would be rough. I'm scared. Jules, I'm going to be out of work for a while."

I could see where his mind was going—finances, work, not being able to care for his family. These were his worries on a normal day. The cancer had just amplified them.

"Jeff, look at me. We will figure this out. I know you are worried but we have options and I will be here to help you."

He half-smiled. "Jeff, we got through this before and we will get through it again." I squeezed his hand.

"Jules, this is a lot different. Ten years ago I had surgery and that was it. I didn't have to go through chemotherapy. I had the surgery and then got on with my life. I missed one week of work. This is a lot harder. I have no idea if I will even get back to work."

He was right. This was going to be different as he filled me in on more of what Dr. Duffy shared.

"I will need to schedule appointments for iron infusions, a port placement, PET scan, chemotherapy teaching, chemotherapy, pulmonary consults, and pulmonary function tests."

This was all new to us. We didn't experience this ten years ago.

The hardest thing we faced back then was the possibility of not being able to have children and Jeff undergoing surgery that threatened his manhood.

My heart hurt.

Jeff would need three to four cycles of chemotherapy. One cycle was 21 days. The first five days of each chemotherapy cycle would be six hours long. He would be at the clinic Monday through Friday. I wouldn't be allowed to sit with him during his treatments. This was a new policy put into place since the pandemic. He would get the weekend off and then head back into the clinic for more chemotherapy on day eight and day 15.

At the end of each cycle, he would then schedule an appointment for pulmonary function tests (PFTs). These tests showed how well Jeff's lungs were working. Dr. Duffy mentioned that the one drug was really strong and it could permanently damage his lungs. Jeff was not happy about this but what were his options?

Dr. Duffy did say if they started to notice changes then he would need to switch the drug but it wouldn't be as effective at curing the cancer. Hearing the word cure didn't reassure me or make me feel better. Instead, the word made me upset and tense. I'd heard that word before and now look where we were.

I closed my eyes and took some deep breaths.

He mentioned some of the side effects of the treatment. Nausea and vomiting were the main concerns as well as significant fatigue and decreased ability to fight off colds and illnesses. This was an issue as COVID-19 was still a concern. The doctor mentioned we would try to stay on schedule but if his blood work was off before each cycle then chemotherapy would be postponed until his numbers looked better.

Jeff continued, "He wants to start treatment in February. He is scheduling me for a PET scan, blood work to check my iron levels, and a chemotherapy teaching session so we have some education on what to expect. He will schedule an appointment for me to have a port placed in my chest for the chemotherapy drugs."

Jeff was going on and on while my mind was somewhere else. *How will I navigate this with the kids? What will I tell them?*

Do I use the word cancer? They associated that word with dying. I recall the conversation Delaney and I had just last week— "Mom the kids at school said people with cancer die, isn't that sad."

How ironic she heard this just days before we found out about Jeff being diagnosed.

Do I tell them it's seminoma or say Dad is sick and needs special treatment? Do I say he has cancer and sit with what comes up and the questions they have?

Ten years ago, when it was just the two of us, unmarried, facing Jeff's cancer diagnosis, things seemed easier in some ways. But I know it was still tremendously difficult - the possibility of infertility, the urgent surgery Jeff required. We had major decisions to make under pressure, with no time to spare. The experience of confronting Jeff's cancer, while rushed and stressful, brought us closer together. Though now with two children our life was more complex, I would never wish this crisis on anyone else. What we went through together a decade ago united us as a couple.

I'm praying the Lord will give me the words and the courage when the time comes to tell Brindsley and Delaney. I will trust He will guide and navigate this challenge with me.

* * *

I couldn't believe it came back. Jeff did everything right. He had CT Scans for the first five years after his surgery to make sure nothing spread and followed up with the doctors every six months for the last ten years. Jeff recently told me that his urologist whom he first saw in 2011 said to him, "This can come back, don't let your health go and stay on your appointments." I didn't know he said that to Jeff. All I heard from his oncologist was "It won't come back, he's cured."

Well, here we were in 2022 facing this again. I was dreading the thought of telling Brindsley and Delaney —*honesty is the best policy*. Yet I wasn't ready. I needed time to practice what and how much to tell them. I wanted to use the right words and be calm and positive. Positive about cancer? Sigh…

I connected with their school counselor. My concern was that if their behavior changed, I wanted their teachers to have a heads-up. If they started to notice the kids were having a hard time I wanted to give them some extra support. I called the school counselor and filled her in on what was going on. She was wonderful and very supportive. She agreed to talk with them and was glad to be a resource for us. She encouraged me to keep her posted once I told the kids. She would then schedule a time to check-in.

Brindsley had started to notice something was up with Jeff. It was hard to hide, his weight loss, lack of appetite, and need for more sleep. We had a Nerf basketball net set up in our bedroom that they played most evenings after dinner.

"It's been a while since Dad has wanted to play."

"I know Brindsley. Dad is not feeling well and we are getting him the care to figure out what is going on."

My heart hurt as I gave him a big hug. "I'm sorry he isn't feeling well right now, I would be happy to play with you." I knew it wasn't the same. He didn't want me, he wanted his dad. I found myself playing many basketball games with him in our bedroom.

We would make up teams. He would stop me every once in a while, "Hey Mom, what's the score of your game." I smiled and most of the time made up a number because I would lose track. Not Brindsley. He was keeping track of his team and the score very diligently. I loved his enthusiasm and enjoyed our time together. Delaney would pop in to watch or cheer us on when her nose wasn't in a book.

I did my best to meet my children's needs during this time. I would be lying if I told you it was easy. The burden of not knowing how to address this with them was heavy on my heart. I felt like I was carrying this alone. I lost sleep. I ruminated about how to approach the situation. I wanted to pretend it wasn't happening. *Maybe I'll wake up and realize this was all a dream.*

I wanted to find the perfect words or the perfect time to tell them their Dad had cancer. Yet we all know, don't we, that perfect doesn't exist. I would need to face this and trust the Lord was with me.

It's Your Move:

Plank on Forearms (Full and Modified)
Check out the It's Your Move channel: www.youtube.com/@juliebhughes

CHAPTER 11

JOYS AND CONCERNS

Where would you like to escape to?

The woods.
Mighty trees stand firm
an army to protect me.
Branches extend over
the giant sky—
A shield from the
commotion.

a birdsong,
the wind
crunch, crunch
with each footfall
quiets the
internal clamor
Solitude—
my sword.

Why don't I like attention?

I asked myself this question as we drove home from church. I didn't like how I responded just minutes ago yet I wasn't prepared.

Jeff announced to everyone his health challenge during joys and concerns. I wasn't ready for the announcement. I was taken off guard when the pastor invited Jeff upfront to be prayed over. In all the churches I'd attended, this was the first time I'd experienced the pastor inviting someone up front. I was accustomed to sitting in the pew and praying. I was surprised by the invitation. Jeff was not. He got right up, walked to the front of the congregation, and stood next to the pastor.

Wow, good for Jeff until the Pastor also invited me. I froze.

I didn't want to stand up in front of everyone. *Why can't we just pray for him where we are?* Jeff was already up there surrounded by some of the church members and I was still standing in the back my stomach clenched. I was upset. I didn't want to do this. I didn't want to go up there. Guilt consumed me as my mind raced, *you need to support him, you need to go up there, what is your problem?*

I didn't know what the problem was but I couldn't move. One lady across the pew stared at me with kind dark eyes. Her mask hid the words though I could read her eyes urging me to move, to go. My legs were like jello. I was holding back tears. *This is for him, not me. Why would the pastor ask me to come up there?*

Jeff was now surrounded by most of the congregation when I finally moved out of the pew and took a place in the back of the crowd. I stood next to someone else and placed my hand on their shoulder. I couldn't get to Jeff, but I wasn't going to push through everyone to make that happen.

Guilt, fear, shame, and anger seeped into my heart. The old story of *what is wrong with me, I wish I was like someone else, and why don't I feel like I belong* replayed in my mind. I knew this feeling. I didn't like it. I wanted to start the morning over.

After the closing hymn, I dashed out of the pew to gather the kids from Sunday school. I didn't want to listen to the story over and over as Jeff began talking to folks. Of course, they had questions and wanted to know more. They were concerned and cared.

My inner judge, Aunt Phoebe scolded me, "You're a crappy wife and a jerk for not standing up there with Jeff." I went to the bathroom and cried— the first real cry since we learned of Jeff's diagnosis. The crying helped release some emotions. Yet I still felt lingering guilt about what had happened just moments before.

I prayed— *Dear Lord, please help me. Please give me the strength to push out the enemy, please protect my mind, and guard my heart. Amen.*

Brindsley and Delaney were happy when I came to gather them from Sunday school. Claudette, their teacher, was sitting at the table with them. Her silver hair shined as the sun peeked through the windows and her warm smile softened my heart. I was so grateful the kids had her during this time. They were focused on their projects, talking, and laughing. I took a seat next to them as they finished up their craft.

Once we picked up, we headed to the front of the church to find Jeff. He was gathered around a few church members having a conversation. I figured we would wait in the car. Before we made it out of the building one of the ladies stopped me. She looked at me concerned, "Julie set this all down at the foot of the cross. Don't turn back to pick it up, give it to Jesus." I nodded and thanked her.

It was exactly what I needed to hear. Many times in my life I would hand over my worries, anxieties, and burdens to Jesus but found myself picking them up again. My reason— *I can do it better. I can handle it myself. I don't need Him.* Instead of trusting Him. Trusting in His plan and promises. Trusting He would see me through.

As I drove us home, I asked myself another question— What just happened? Why did I respond that way? I turned to curiosity instead of beating myself up. I shifted my thoughts from, what was wrong with me to what was I afraid of. *How do I want to show up in this season?*

I got home and took time to write, to answer these questions. Writing was a practice I was happy I turned to. It gave me space to process my feelings about this challenge and it allowed me to decide how I wanted to show up.

I didn't want to be angry towards Jeff and our circumstances. I didn't want to be fearful or anxious about the future. I wanted to choose joy even in the mess. I wanted to find peace and ease even when I didn't know what tomorrow would bring.

I wanted to encourage, pray, and support Jeff and my family. I wanted to give each other grace as we navigate this season together. I would stand firm in my faith and not hide— *to trust in the Lord with all my heart, with all my soul, with all my mind, and with all my strength.*

It's Your Move:

Release the Butterfly and Kick the Sky

Check out the It's Your Move channel: www.youtube.com/@juliebhughes

CHAPTER 12

HEROES

Jeff received a call we were praying for— his iron infusion bumped up two days sooner than expected. Dr. Duffy was hopeful the infusion would help Jeff feel better going into chemotherapy treatment. I was relieved we could get this process started. We needed something to give Jeff the ambition to keep his chin up. *Thank you, Lord, for another answered prayer.*

I entered the clinic with Jeff, both of us wearing a mask. Masks were mandatory indoors. The nurse at the front entrance stopped me and asked to see my COVID-19 vaccination card. I panicked as I opened my wallet praying I didn't take it out. Phew, I handed it to her and she let me inside. She reminded me I would need to show her this card every time I came in.

What if I didn't get the vaccine? Would that mean I wouldn't be allowed inside? I was thankful I didn't need to worry about those questions swirling in my mind.

While Jeff was getting his infusion, I found a comfy chair to sit on. I had an hour and a half to wait. I would use this time to write. I needed the page to empty my worries, thoughts, and what-ifs. I needed the page to see what negative affirmations were taking up space in my mind. I was willing to shift those to something helpful instead.

As I looked up from my notebook, I noticed so many folks coming and going. I wondered what they were here for today. I wondered if they were getting better. My heart hurt thinking about the challenges they were facing. We all were facing.

Life can be so painful and yet we must find a way to keep going. I returned to the page and wrote one word at the top— Heroes. Each person who walked through these clinic doors. Each caregiver who sat in the waiting room. Each patient who endured scans, blood work, infusions, chemotherapy— *Heroes.*

* * *

Jeff came out with a pep in his step. His mask slipped down resting under his nose. I smiled. His eyes squinted as he headed my way. I was surprised— *does the infusion work this fast? Heck, I'm going with it, I believe in the placebo effect.* I was building him up with that in mind. I was happy to see him in a better headspace after his treatment as we walked out of the clinic.

He mentioned they wanted him to come back in a week for another round. *I hope it starts to make him feel better. He is still so tired and pale. Will he be ready to start chemotherapy?* I noticed my thoughts. Aunt Phoebe, my inner judge, trying to squeak in with her fear tactics. I took a deep breath— *we've got a great team in our corner.* I trusted Dr. Duffy and knew he wouldn't set him up for chemotherapy if he didn't think Jeff could handle it. I grabbed Jeff's hand as we walked to the car.

We are ready to face this next challenge together.

My mom picked up the kids from school and brought them back to our house. I was happy my mom was available to help us out. I didn't like to rush. This was helpful to have my mom step in. We may need her more as Jeff's appointments fill up the calendar. I would need to encourage myself to ask her for help and not feel bad about it.

As we got closer to home, I mentioned the children. "I think we need to tell them something more." Jeff agreed. I told him I would start the conversation. I was thinking of not using the word cancer unless I needed to. I wanted to stay calm and positive.

The positive bit was more for me. I didn't want to break down and cry which if I did, hey I'm human but I wanted to stay strong for our children. I wanted them to know that everything would be okay. When we arrived home the kids were at the kitchen table having a snack with my mom. I thanked my mom for picking them up. She smiled and nodded.

We sat down with them. I figured this was the best time. Here goes…*please Lord give me the right words to say.*

"Brindsley and Delaney, we know why Dad's iron has been so low, why he has been so tired and unable to play with you. He has seminoma and will need chemotherapy to treat it."

They both stopped eating when they heard the word chemotherapy. They looked at me then at Jeff. Delaney's face changed and I hurried in with, "He is going to be fine. We love you both so much. We will take care of you."

Delaney began to cry.

Brindsley shouted, "Why did this happen now dad can't play basketball with me!"

"We know it's hard but he will get better and will soon be back to playing with you Brindsley."

Delaney ran to her room and shut the door. Jeff got up from the table and went in to be with her. I stayed at the table with Brindsley and my mom. I asked if he had any other questions.

"What else is on your mind?" He didn't respond. I could tell he was upset. He didn't say anything more as he finished his snack. I was surprised they didn't ask me what seminoma was. I was planning on them bombarding me with questions but they didn't.

Perhaps hearing the word chemotherapy was enough. I gave Brindsley and Delaney space to process this information.

I got up and grabbed the yellow LIVESTRONG bracelets. I thought maybe this would be helpful. Delaney and Jeff came back out to the kitchen and I handed one to each of them. I never took mine off from 2011. I told the kids we were going to wear these bracelets to stay strong for each other and Dad.

Delaney started to smile and wiped the tears from her cheeks. She placed the yellow bracelet on her wrist, "This is cool."

I had everyone place their hands in a team huddle with the bracelets showing. I had no idea what I was doing but went with it. I wanted to bring up everyone's spirits. We were going to need something to keep us united through this challenge ahead.

On the count of three…one…two…three…Hughes Strong!

It's Your Move:

Superhero Glasses

Check out the It's Your Move channel: www.youtube.com/@juliebhughes

CHAPTER 13

MENTAL PING PONG

When we found out Jeff's diagnosis and treatment plan I hesitated to tell my friends and family. *Do I want them to know what we're going through? Is it too much to share?* I didn't want them to feel sorry for me or treat me differently. Of course, I couldn't control how they reacted to the news but I could decide if I wanted to tell them or not.

Fear showed up.

I didn't want to call each person individually and tell them the news over and over. Would a group text be okay? Would that be the right way to handle this situation?

Guilt showed up.

Mental ping-pong was exhausting.

What if they wanted to help? *I don't need help. I can handle this. I'm not the one who is sick.*

Julie, this will be good practice for you. This kind thought slipped in. I was surprised and grateful. I would like to practice asking for help. I would like to break this pattern of keeping troubles only to myself.

What if I asked my close friends? What if I told them I have no idea what I need but this is what we are facing? How would they respond?

I would find out. I would let them know. I sent a text to my siblings and several of my close friends and shared the news. I apologized up front for not calling each one individually yet I was hopeful they understood. I was hopeful they would want to know.

It wasn't long before messages were popping up on my phone. I was nervous to read their responses. What a shock this must be to receive via text— *I should've called each friend and each sibling instead. There I go again with the "shoulds."*

Thankfully, the messages were filled with kindness, love, and understanding. I was relieved. They would be our support near and far even though I didn't know yet what that would look like.

Family and friends swooped in with cards, packages, meals, coffee, and fun gifts and games for our children. I did not expect this. I felt uncomfortable by it all. I was aware of my negative thoughts and self-sabotage. *I don't need anyone's help.* I discovered through many years of therapy this thought only created more isolation, not connection.

* * *

I grew up with the mindset of—do it yourself. *Don't ask for help. Don't be a burden to others and for goodness sake don't share difficult or uncomfortable circumstances with anyone.* I was taught individualism over community. I took pride in my self-reliance. I still do yet over the years I began to question this one-sided way of thinking. *What if I was a part of a community and my self-reliance was welcome too?*

Writing was one of my tools for self-care to help me de-stress, process my thoughts and feelings, and face the negative self-talk swirling in my mind. I refused to go back into my old unhealthy patterns of hiding and not accepting help. *What did I do?* I wrote. I wrote to help me see what I was holding on to.

Why do I believe I don't belong with others? Why do I like to hide? Why am I gripped so tight to this independence? These questions covered my notebook.

It's interesting what happens when you start writing things on the page. I experienced a synchronicity moment— an email landed in my inbox to join an Akimbo Workshop called Writing in Community (WIC). I took the hint and signed up in March of 2021.

I was oblivious as to how this online community would answer my questions but I wanted to write a book so I moved forward with that goal, not expecting any answers. I had no idea what would unfold by showing up each day. I found my courage and introduced myself to other members, folks I'd never met. I shared my writing and commented on what others were writing.

I was uncomfortable but wanted to contribute. I was paying attention to how to do this. I was surprised by my willingness. I began making connections and finding the others.

I was beginning to feel like I belonged even with my lack of writing skills. The most important part for me, I felt seen, safe, and cared for as I showed up daily to write.

I noticed the change it was creating in me. I was gaining confidence. I was trying new things. I was even getting better at writing and a self-published book was on the horizon.

My thoughts shifted to "Julie, you are someone worth knowing" and "You do belong here."

I was willing to put myself out there and the response was kindness, support, and encouragement. Keep writing. Keep going.

When Jeff's diagnosis came in 2022, I felt secure enough to share what was happening with my writing community. I wasn't planning on writing about this, I had a book to write, but I found myself unable to focus on the book. I turned to poetry and this new challenge my family and I now faced. I remember writing it out on the screen after I had my morning pages completed. I hesitated to share such heavy terrible news yet I was met with words of kindness, prayers, and love.

People who I had never met in real life were not afraid to see me, to comfort me. They were teaching me what it meant to be a part of a community. You show up, you don't disappear. You validate and do not ignore. You hold space, you don't hijack it.

I'm forever indebted to you, (writing in community) for keeping me going during this season. You brought me stability, support, and kindness during this difficult time. The friendships I cultivated gave me reassurance to keep showing up and stay connected. I didn't hide. I didn't run. I found courage in our crisis. Thank you for coming alongside me and my family.

* * *

I was speechless when my friend Terri sent me a financial gift via Venmo with a message attached.

"Julie, as discussed, WIC and we want you to use this for parking, incidentals, co-pays, meals, pizza, housekeeping, or what you see fit. We know the many incidentals that others cannot consider. It's the least, collectively, we can do for Jeff and family."

I was shocked when I read the amount. I was not expecting this. My first thought was—*how can I accept this? I can't accept this. Why is it so hard for me to receive a gift?*

Terri sent me a text message to encourage me to accept their gift. I wonder to this day how she knew I would need her encouraging nudge. She continued, "It will help with parking fees, or grab a pizza, or something fun for the kids." I read her words over and over. Astonished by her thoughtfulness, care, and attention. Grateful I was a part of her community.

It brought tears to my eyes knowing how loved we were. Folks whom I'd never met in person but had the pleasure to meet via Zoom in our writing sessions, shared their generosity, prayers, and support. I was overjoyed.

It's Your Move:
Bridge with Pushing the Sky
Check out the It's Your Move channel: www.youtube.com/@juliebhughes

CHAPTER 14

COLOR OF MY THOUGHTS

At the beginning of February, Jeff had his PET scan. I gave him a hug and kiss before he opened the passenger side door. He would text me when to pick him up. I had a terrible thought as I watched him walk into the clinic— *what if his cancer has spread all over?* The thought made me sick and I yelled at myself for it. *Why would you think that Julie?*

I tried hard to shift my thoughts to something helpful or true but that thought lingered. *What if his cancer has spread all over?* I felt sick as I pulled away from the clinic. I turned on the radio. I prayed a song would come on to help distract me—to give me something else to say to myself. Here was my chance to prove I could manage my mind, yet I couldn't shift this thought. I couldn't shake it. I'd been doing the work for several years on questioning and redirecting my thoughts, a daily practice, and yet here I was still a beginner.

I realized at that moment I needed help— quotes, bible verses, and encouraging sentences placed around me. Continuous truths, reminders, and affirmations to protect my mind and guard my heart. When I got home I grabbed my index cards and began to write. I wrote out bible verses my friend sent me, quotes for strength and encouragement, and affirmations to practice and repeat to overcome my negative thoughts.

One quote stood out by Marcus Aurelius, "Your soul takes on the color of your thoughts."

My soul was black and it was making me sick. I would not let the dark win. I would not let my soul stay in the black. I had the power and choice of where to direct my thinking.

I wanted my soul to be blue. The ocean or sky— wide open and calm. Full of possibility. I wanted my soul to be light. *I am yellow—dandelions in a country field as I run past.* The colors of sunshine, bananas, and gold. I feel warmth and optimism.

This 15-minute writing exercise changed everything. I felt empowered. I had my armor of cards to guide me. I had the colors I wanted to be. I taped the white index cards in the kitchen, bathroom, and my car. The places I would be most.

I began washing dishes. I stopped to read some of the verses I taped along the window sill. I felt at peace. My mind was calm as I continued scrubbing the pots and pans repeating the verse—

"So do not fear, for I am with you; do not be dismayed, for I am your God. I will strengthen you and help you; I will uphold you with my righteous right hand." Isaiah 41:10

* * *

Jeff was standing outside waiting for me after his PET scan. He got in the car and the first words out of his mouth were "I'm radioactive. I need to keep my distance from you and the kids."

"Are you kidding?"

"No."

"Okay." He was serious.

"They told me I shouldn't put the kids to bed tonight or be close to them until tomorrow, no hugs."

I didn't see this coming. Did they mention this and I just don't remember?

"Hmm…okay."

I let it go. No point in getting upset about it. I was learning to pivot. I reasoned more practice was a good thing.

When the kids got home from school I tried to come up with some superhero happy twist— yet failed. My capacity to think on the fly was not happening. I gave it to them straight, "We need to keep our distance from Dad just until tomorrow morning. He had a test done that made him radioactive, and we don't want to be in close contact with the radiation. I'll put you both to bed tonight."

Their eyes widened, "Whoa, okay."

They didn't need anything more and went off to play. I was grateful my kids were reminding me I didn't have to try so hard. I didn't need to pretend this wasn't happening. I didn't need to put a positive spin on every single thing.

This was difficult for me as a mother— it was hard to see my children disappointed, sad, and worried— yet these emotions were all a part of life. It wasn't my job to shield them or deny them their feelings. It was my job to listen and give them a safe place to land. I prayed I was showing up in this way.

* * *

When we met with Dr. Duffy to go over the results of the PET scan he shared that the cancer spread to some lymph nodes and the duodenum. He was very optimistic that the chemotherapy would cure his cancer if it was seminoma. He was waiting on a few more pathologists to examine his biopsy. It was the duodenum that was throwing everyone off and keeping them on their toes.

This was a weird place for seminoma to spread. The doctors in our care were working hard for us. I hoped through Jeff's unusual case they would learn and grow to help someone else. At least we were keeping things interesting.

Dr. Duffy wanted to wait to start treatment until he heard from the pathologist. He didn't want this coming back and they needed to get the right treatment drugs to accomplish this. "The goal is a cure," I believe that's what he said.

When I heard the word cure I was surprised by my reaction. Instead of jumping up and down and hugging the doctor, I was upset. My stomach clenched and my chest tightened. I sat in silence. I thought I would be relieved to hear that instead, I was uneasy. I heard this before when Jeff was first diagnosed in 2011.

What does he mean by cure? This was the question I wished I asked in 2011. This was the question I shoved down even in Dr. Duffy's office. I couldn't find the courage to ask. Instead, I blurted out from underneath my mask, "What about his brain?"

I hope I didn't sound rude but I remember Jeff telling me his family history was prevalent with cancer. I wanted to make sure it hadn't spread to his brain. I thought the PET scan checked the brain but it didn't. This was where my focus had been since we learned of his diagnosis.

Dr. Duffy nodded and validated my concern. He ordered an MRI to scan Jeff's brain to make sure all was clear since the PET scan did not check this area. I was relieved. Dr. Duffy scheduled the MRI on the 16th of February, two days after the port placement.

I looked at the calendar for the weeks ahead— each day filled with at least one appointment. Jeff did his best to schedule them when the children were in school. It wasn't always possible. We were grateful to my mom and his parents who lived nearby to help us.

We had a second opinion scheduled with Sloan Kettering at the end of the week. We let Dr. Duffy know and he was pleased. It was his recommendation. I'd been so exhausted I didn't know if I had the energy to drive to New York City and back. Of course, I would do it if it was needed, however, we were hopeful we could meet with the oncologist via telehealth.

I would trust in the Lord to give me strength. I was praying we could have the treatment here. I was hopeful we wouldn't need to travel.

After our morning visit with Dr. Duffy, we drove to the other side of town for Jeff's chemotherapy teaching appointment. During this appointment, we learned what Jeff should expect during treatment and the side effects of the drugs. There were a lot of side effects which made me concerned, a stack of papers with all of what could happen.

I tried to keep a poker face as the nurse practitioner shared the long list of vomiting, nausea, fatigue, night sweats, mouth sores, neuropathy of hands and feet, muscle pain, headaches, dizziness, and hearing changes. The list went on. We listened. We sat there together and took it in.

I found myself tense up as she continued to spew out all the information. She handed us packets of papers to read through and things to consider that I wouldn't even think about. Why would I, we never have gone through this exact experience.

The oncology nurse explained that once Jeff's chemotherapy started, he would need to take special precautions at home. Specifically, he must close the toilet lid and flush twice after every use. At first, this sounded odd to me, but she explained it was because the chemo drugs exit the body through waste, so flushing thoroughly prevented exposure to others in the home. I made sure to write down these instructions, as we'd need to be very careful during treatment.

She recommended picking fruit without bruises or marks, making sure Jeff's food was thoroughly cleaned and cooked, avoiding foods that could cause food poisoning, and having your well water tested before treatment started to make sure there weren't any contaminants in your water.

It was a lot to think about. They say 'knowledge is power' however I didn't feel much power knowing all of this. I felt overwhelmed and incompetent.

I found myself on my hands and knees that day scrubbing the bathroom floors, cabinets, shower, and bathtub, something I admit I hadn't done in a while. Dusting off the tops of the cabinets and wiping down the wood paneling with wood polish. I made a mental list in my mind of what to do next...*call the well guy.*

The chemotherapy would be about four months. We would hate to have him stop because of our water being contaminated or household germs. Our goal was to get through the chemotherapy without Jeff getting sick. Looking back this was a high expectation to set as COVID-19 was still a threat, the kids were in school, we were in the middle of winter, and who knew how his body would respond to the treatment. I had to remind myself to focus on what I could control—I suppose that was why I was in the bathroom cleaning.

I could control the cleanliness of our home. It was a great distraction too. I found myself feeling better as I looked at the floor sparkle. *I can do this.* Then reality hit me in the face like a ton of bricks.

Would I have the energy and motivation to clean the bathroom like this every day? Could I truly keep the germs away?

I sat on the bathroom floor. My tears landed on the white porcelain. I was grateful Jeff didn't hear me. I let the tears come then I picked myself up and got back to work. I had a phone call to make.

Even though we just had our water tested one year ago I was worried. I got on the phone after my cleaning frenzy to schedule a time for them to test the water, and change our filtration system— I wanted peace of mind. The man on the other end seemed like he was trying to talk me out of it, which I appreciated. It wasn't cheap, but I mentioned Jeff's diagnosis so he would understand why I wanted this done again.

He heard me. He would send a guy out the next day. Another task crossed off my list.

It's Your Move:
Cat-Camel
Check out the It's Your Move channel: www.youtube.com/@juliebhughes

CHAPTER 15

THE PLAYLIST

My heart sick
stomach in knots
I drive alone
a song comes on.

How did she know
what song to send
to pull me out
of the darkness
to clear my head.

How did she know
the music to
shift my mood.
To bring my chin up and
change my view.

I'm feeling angry
I'm feeling sad—
I turn up the volume
and don't feel
as bad.
My fingers
tap the wheel,
my voice
bounces along,
I refuse

to think about
all that is wrong.

The exact melody
to soften my pain
I find myself singing,
humming—
we're going to be
okay.

My friend Carrie-Anne was a rock star at texting me songs to keep me going during Jeff's health challenge. Bob Marley's quote, "One good thing about music, when it hits you, you feel no pain," came to mind as I turned up the volume to the latest song Carrie-Anne had sent.

I don't know how she managed to know the exact song I needed, but she did. I saved each one to return to when I wanted to change my focus, find joy, or soften my pain.

I sang my heart out— some days with tears in my eyes, some days with laughter. When the pain, sadness, or overwhelm consumed me the playlist gave me strength, peace, and hope. It lifted me.

The songs she sent, some of which were from our days together in college, brought back happy memories. My mind was back at Bloomsburg University— running alongside her or hanging out in the library studying. (we cherished the library...don't ask me why.)

Music was a way for me to find joy in this terrible season. I was grateful for Carrie-Anne to remind me each day. Even though she was miles away, she was with me in the backseat when I dropped Jeff off at his treatments. She was in the passenger seat when I went to pick him up. She was in the kitchen with me dancing when I didn't know what else to do. What an incredible gift. What an amazing friend.

It's Your Move:
Dance Party— Turn the Volume Up
Check out the It's Your Move channel: www.youtube.com/@juliebhughes

CHAPTER 16

BAD LUCK

Jeff's case was very unusual and why Dr. Duffy wanted him to get a second opinion. The word unusual made me feel nervous and uneasy. The story I started to tell myself was his cancer wouldn't respond to treatment.

Oh brain, why do you go right to the worst-case scenario? Why do I want to repeat that story to myself? It was only making me feel more anxious and scared. Jeff and I were seated at the kitchen table. The laptop in front of us. We were meeting the doctor from Sloan Kettering and thankful he agreed to a telehealth session.

Neither Jeff nor I felt up for the five-hour drive to New York City. As we waited for the doctor to appear on the video screen, I squirmed anxiously in my chair, wondering what this new doctor would tell us. Now that Jeff's diagnosis of seminoma was confirmed, I hoped we were in good hands with Dr. Duffy. My preference was to pursue local treatment options for Jeff if possible, rather than going to New York City.

When the doctor finally showed up on the screen I kept quiet. Jeff began sharing his story and the doctor listened on the other end. When it was the doctor's turn to speak he mentioned he was surprised the cancer returned and the location.

The fact that the seminoma came back and spread to the duodenum was very unusual. It came back after ten years. It showed up in an odd location in Jeff's body and wasn't identified a year ago when he had an upper endoscopy. I wondered if there was something we could have done to prevent this. Was there something that triggered this that we had control over?

My mind raced with questions—*Does it mean this will be harder to treat? Does this mean he will need more chemotherapy than they have planned? Will the chemotherapy work?*

Why did this come back?

This one thought turned over and over—*why did this come back*, as I sat in the chair trying to pay attention to what the doctor was saying. I zoned out until I heard, "It's just bad luck."

Could he hear my thoughts? I stared at the computer screen wanting to hug him. This one sentence calmed my mind— "It's just bad luck."

Then he continued, "I've seen a few cases of testicular cancer spread to the duodenum but not many. The ones I've seen responded well to chemotherapy."

When he told us that my body relaxed, okay—*yes, Jeff's case is unusual and he will respond to chemotherapy.* I would tell myself this story instead. Jeff was going to make it through this and we were on the right track in regards to treatment.

The doctor from Sloan Kettering agreed with Dr. Duffy's treatment plan. He reassured us— "If Jeff was my patient we would do the same chemotherapy drugs." He mentioned he would do four cycles to be sure they got it all. We were happy we could stay here and work with Dr. Duffy.

The doctor mentioned they were researching patients if Jeff would be willing to participate. They wanted to understand testicular cancer more and examine the DNA in families with this cancer type. Jeff agreed to participate in the study.

Sloan Kettering would call Jeff with the next steps. In the meantime, Jeff set up genetic testing through the cancer clinic. This would help them identify if Jeff was susceptible to other cancers. It would also give us more information if something genetically had been passed to our children.

Brindsley was on our minds. His risk was four to five times greater to develop this cancer. We were praying this would not pass to him. We were praying it stopped with Jeff.

* * *

Bad Luck

I ran with Felicia on Saturday for 90 minutes at Onondaga Lake Park. We got heavy snow the night before and the roads in Manlius were not yet cleared. I was grateful Onondaga Lake Park was an option in the winter.

I stepped out of my car. It was so quiet. I love that about a big snowstorm. The snow brings silence. It brings me peace. My mind was calm and my body followed. As we walked through the snow we noticed the snowplow hadn't made its way through yet. Oh well, we started anyway even though it was slow. We laughed as we slogged in the ankle-deep snow.

When we turned around to head back the plow was out—fantastic, a path. It was a little slick but gave us a chance to pick up the pace. I didn't have much energy though. Maybe it was from the week, Jeff had a lot of doctor's appointments, the kids had been a little down, and I was worried about finances.

Do I try to work outside the home to get a little money coming in? Who would take Jeff to his appointments every day? What about the kids?

I shook off those thoughts confident that we would find a way.

I had so many questions.

Why can't we access our retirement accounts to pay our bills and expenses? It's our money and we're in a crisis. Why do we need to wait until a certain age? How interesting our system is—save the money for when you're older. I get it but when you're in a true emergency why are we not allowed to touch our own money?

I turned my focus back to my breath, back to the snow covered lake. Grateful to be able to run. Grateful that I could still slip out of the house in the early morning even though Jeff was sick. He wanted me to go. He reassured me he would be okay for the few hours I was gone. Brindsley and Delaney would be okay too.

I was grateful. Running nourished my soul.

It's Your Move:
Mobility Movements
Check out the It's Your Move channel: www.youtube.com/@juliebhughes

CHAPTER 17

SWEET AND TOUGH

Apple slices lend
A sweet crunch when life is tough
Hint of cinnamon

Jeff was scheduled to have his medical port placed on February 14th. Happy Valentine's Day to us. They explained that the port would be placed under the skin at the upper part of his chest. This would be used for his treatments and blood draws. A convenient way to access Jeff's vein without the constant needle pokes. He was grateful.

I figured I needed to have another talk with the kids. I wanted them to be prepared when they saw this quarter-size protrusion in Jeff's upper chest. It would also be an opportunity to circle back about the school counselor.

I chose the kitchen table and gathered them around with snacks after school. I didn't know what I was doing but reasoned this news was best shared with food.

Deep breath.

"Brindsley and Delaney I want you to know that the school counselor is available to talk with you anytime you need her."

Brindsley's blue eyes met mine, "Why would we go and talk to her, because of Dad?"

"Yes, if you would like someone else besides me and Dad, she will be another person you can talk with."

"Okay" as he started on another apple slice.

"Dad will be starting treatment soon and he will have this little device placed in his chest, under his skin. It will help his care team give him the medicine he needs to get rid of the seminoma."

I was doing my best to sidestep the "C" word.

"What is seminoma?" Delaney set down her apple slice and turned her eyes towards mine.

Deep breath.

The question I'd been dreading.

"It's a type of cancer. The type Dad has is treatable and curable. Dad is going to be okay."

She stared at me, "But I thought if you get cancer you die."

"No honey, there are many types of cancer and many are curable. Dad has one of those types. He isn't going to die."

She looked relieved, "That's good" and went back to eating.

Brindsley didn't say anything while we sat gathered around the table. All I could hear was the crunch of their apples. I watched them eat while Aunt Phoebe, my inner judge, squeaked in with her nonsense. "Is that all you're going to tell them? You better be right that this is curable, wonder if it's not."

Deep breath.

I was determined to not let fear get in the way of how I showed up for my children. I closed my eyes and said a small prayer— *Dear Lord please guard my heart and protect my mind. I need your guidance.*

I fixed my eyes back on my children.

"Do you have any other questions?"

I heard in unison "No."

"Okay, but please know that you can ask us anything at any time. Your questions will never be met with anger or avoidance."

They both nodded and then went off to play together.

Deep breath.

I was happy they had each other.

Looking back I was happy they asked questions and we encouraged it. We didn't want them to hold this in and that was why I offered the school counselor as another person to help them carry the load. These difficult conversations went better than I expected. I thanked the Lord, grateful I had Him to guide me.

It's Your Move:
Hip Dips and Press-Ups
Check out the It's Your Move channel: www.youtube.com/@juliebhughes

CHAPTER 18

HAPPY VALENTINE'S DAY

The first stop was to drop off Brindsley and Delaney at school and then bring Jeff to the hospital. Today he would be getting his port placed in his chest. I reminded the kids I would be picking them up after school. Jeff reassured me his procedure was quick and he would be done around lunchtime.

Perfect. The plan was set, and maybe Jeff and I would have some time together before I picked up the kids. It was Valentine's Day, not like I was keeping track or anything.

We hugged and kissed the kids goodbye before they opened the car door.

"Have a great day. We love you."

"Love you too!" they shouted before closing the car doors.

I pulled up to the hospital around 9:30 a.m.

"I'll call you when to come back and pick me up." Jeff kissed me on the cheek and I hugged him.

"Okay, I love you."

"I love you too, Jules."

I watched him walk in through the double glass sliding doors through my rearview mirror before I headed back home. I prayed the procedure would go well.

I had my running clothes on so I wouldn't neglect my six-mile run. I noticed some mornings I couldn't get out of bed at my usual 5 a.m. run time. I was so tired. I didn't know why since I was still going to bed at 9 p.m. Of course, looking back I know why— my brain energy was on this new health challenge Jeff was facing and being available and aware of my children's needs and questions.

I pulled into the driveway and took off on foot to the country roads. I faced the biting wind and thought about Jeff. *I can face this cold, Jeff is facing "C"! Come on Julie, this is nothing. I can do this. I want to do this.*

I straightened my arms down by my side and shook them out hoping that would relax my mind, refocus, and keep me going. The wind continued, it wouldn't let up. One foot before the other, breathe, relax, and run. I continued with those words to fuel me as I took in the snow-covered fields.

Running was my go-to and a way to carry the loads of life…especially the ones we don't see coming. I used movement to keep going through this challenge and to get out of my head. I turned to my notebook. I wrote daily to work through my anger, sadness, and loss. I wrote poems to help me process my emotions.

During this time, I noticed more and more and paid attention to the simple things. I didn't want to get sucked down in the muck or let this diagnosis steal my joy, peace, or hope.

Of course, my mind would tell me the opposite. Aunt Phoebe squeaked in, "You can't find joy, peace, or hope during this time. This is terrible, this is brutal!"

Yes, it was terrible and brutal, but the longer I stayed in those thoughts, the more anger, despair, and sadness would creep into my heart and soul. I didn't want to show up for my family with that energy.

And we all know we have control over how we show up no matter the circumstance. Yet, it's easy to forget.

* * *

When I came into the house around 11 a.m. I rushed to my phone to see if Jeff texted. Sure enough, his name was displayed as I swiped to retrieve what he wrote.

"I'm still waiting, they had an emergency. I might be here awhile."

GRR. I felt bad. He had been waiting there since 9:30 a.m. and couldn't eat until the procedure was finished. He must be starving, or maybe not. His appetite was still off.

I texted back, "Okay, I'm sorry this is turning into a long day."

"It's fine, I'm watching TV."

A graphics interchange format (GIF) of The Big Lebowski came next. I couldn't help but laugh. That movie was so strange but super funny. I was happy Jeff seemed so laid back about the entire situation. I jumped in the shower, ate, and started work. I finally got a text around 1:30 p.m.

"They are taking me in now. I'll text you when I'm ready to be picked up."

I continued with the plan of collecting the kids from school and anticipated them coming along with me to the hospital. I finally got a call around 4:30 p.m. "Your husband did great, you can come get him now."

Wow! A short procedure took an entire day and instead of getting bent out of shape I was relieved it went well. The kids were not delighted when I told them they needed to get back in the car.

"Mom, we are playing a good game."

"Can't you just leave us home?"

"No, I'm not going to leave you home. Grab some books and let's go. It's not that far of a drive and Dad will be so happy to see us all."

"Oh, alright." they both grumbled.

I watched as they grabbed a few books, a stuffed animal, and a notebook with pens. We were ready for the 25-minute drive. I laughed to myself as their arms overflowed with their treasures for the ride.

As I backed out of the garage it dawned on me— *what are we doing for dinner?* My mind searched for what was in the refrigerator. *What did I make last night? What did we have last night?* I couldn't remember. *What can I throw together?*

A mile down the road, the light bulb finally came on— *Oh, that's right my friend dropped off a meal to us last night and we have plenty still in the fridge.* I let out a breath, smiled at my friend's thoughtfulness, and headed to the hospital with the weight of dinner figured out…leftovers.

We pulled up outside the hospital. A nurse was heading our way pushing Jeff in a wheelchair. He stood with caution and eased into the passenger seat. He smiled and apologized for the delay. I placed my hand on his shoulder, "Jeff, we are just happy to see you," and kissed him on the cheek.

"Hi, Dad! How'd it go?" Brindsley and Delaney leaned forward from the back seat.

"Hey, kids." A wide smile returned to Jeff's face.

"Good, I'm just a little sore." He had a few papers in his hand with instructions for the next 72 hours. We headed home and Jeff shared a bit of his adventure in the hospital.

When we arrived home he went right to the couch and laid down. I began pulling food out of the refrigerator to reheat dinner. I was hopeful he would eat with us.

I looked at his post-op papers to see how I could help with his discomfort while I started the microwave. Grateful once again for this meal I didn't need to prepare. I was exhausted.

It's Your Move:
Hug Yourself and Roll
Check out the It's Your Move channel: www.youtube.com/@juliebhughes

CHAPTER 19

WINS FOR THE WEEK

I grabbed my notebook and pen. I needed to shift my thoughts and writing was an action to help me. I wrote at the top— *What are my wins this week?*

I began to write. My hand raced across the page— *Jeff's MRI negative— cancer hasn't spread to his brain, laundry folded and put away, meals planned out for the week, water tested and filter changed, laughter (I don't know what Brindsley said but he had me rolling on the ground), wrote a new poem, Jeff's genetic testing results came back negative, and received an email from the children's school counselor.*

Looking at my list of wins did help my mood. Even though we were in a difficult time there was so much to be happy, content, and grateful for. This skill or practice to notice the wins, pay attention to gratitude, and seek joy each day was not lost on me. I had a choice of what to focus on.

I was comforted by the follow-up email the school counselor sent me. I knew she was going to talk to Brindsley and Delaney separately this week but had no idea she already made the time. Her email made my day. Her positive feedback encouraged me that Jeff and I were doing okay through this difficult time.

She wrote:

> "Both seem to be in a good place right now, so I let them know I was here
> if needed and now they know where to find me! I think you both have done
> a great job of talking with them and making them feel safe to ask questions.
> I will be thinking of you all and hoping for good news after treatments."

I wanted my children to feel safe. I wanted them to know I was there and going to take care of them. I was happy she mentioned this in her email. During my childhood there were many moments when I didn't feel safe, reading this meant the world to me as a mother.

When it was time to pick up the kids from school, I was curious if they would mention their time with the school counselor. They didn't. They had a lot to share with me on the drive home but it wasn't about that.

Once we arrived home and settled in with a snack Delaney looked at me, "Mom I talked with the school counselor today."

"Oh, that's great. How did it go?"

"Good, we talked a little bit about Dad and she said she was praying for us." I smiled and hugged her.

"I'm so happy you have someone to talk with at school."

Delaney looked at me with curiosity, "So I can go to her whenever I want?"

"Yes, honey anytime you want."

Delaney smiled. I gave her another hug.

Brindsley was sitting at the table listening. I was waiting to see if he would chime in. He didn't so I turned to him and asked, "How did your time go with the counselor?"

"It was okay. I missed playing with my friends though so I don't want to go again."

"Okay, well maybe you can meet with her at another time."

"No, I would rather play with my friends."

I nodded and didn't press the topic any further. I didn't want to force him to talk yet I wondered if it was bad timing. If she grabbed him during math or science would he be all for it? Would he want to go again? Would a counselor outside of school be better? Do we need that? I was full of questions with no answers.

Deep breath.

One day at a time. I trusted I would know if Brindsley or Delaney needed more support. I would pay attention and link them up with someone when and if the time came. I prayed I would not let fear guide my parenting.

We finished our snack and bundled up in snow pants, hats, and gloves. It was time to play outside and have some fun. I was grateful we had nature to lean on. I was hopeful my children were going to be okay.

What are your wins for the week? Take a moment to write down a few things then get back here to read the rest of the book.

It's Your Move:
Raise It Up
Check out the It's Your Move channel: www.youtube.com/@juliebhughes

CHAPTER 20

MANUFACTURE SUNSHINE™

My friend Terri
is a light-bringer
She reminds me to
look for the nuggets of joy
and to manufacture my
own sunshine.

A wise invitation
as cancer has crept into our home
unwelcomed—
a thief in the night
yet we won't let it
steal our joy
Terri reminds me.

I will keep my head up
I will keep going
I will keep my light bright
for my children
for my husband
even during this terrible time.

I'm given another day
to create
to serve
to manufacture sunshine™.

A Real Ballbuster

Thank you, Terri
for sharing your story—
The Focused Fight
to help mine.

Jeff's first cycle of chemotherapy was scheduled for the same week the kids had off from school. What great timing. GRR. The story I was telling myself was— *the kids can't see Jeff sick, what if he throws up when they are home or he is in awful pain?*

This was not helpful and I was aware. I noticed how much I wanted to protect them from seeing the ugly side of things. Some of which I had no control over. I took a deep breath and questioned— *What if they see Jeff in pain? What if he throws up? How will I handle it? How will I show up?*

These questions changed my view completely. I grabbed my pen and began writing on the page—

They will see empathy. They will see Dad fight back from this. They will see compassion. They will see what it takes to care for someone we love. I will stay calm. I will answer all their questions. They can handle this and so can I.

I found myself leaning into curiosity and uncertainty with less panic. Writing was a powerful tool. I was grateful for my notebooks and a stash of pens.

* * *

I was trying my best to plan out the week with the kids home on winter break. A few of Jeff's treatments started at 7:30 a.m. and I didn't want to bring the kids. I wanted them to have a fun break without dragging them to appointments. I wanted them to have the chance to sleep in (*I laugh at that thought but hey you never know*) and play, not to wake up and drive their dad to chemotherapy all week.

Sigh…*I'm a planner.* It was really hard to plan anything. I had no idea what these next four months were going to look like for us. *Julie, take one day at a time.*

My intention during this season was to be willing to ask for help and receive it with a cheerful heart. Would I practice this week? A gentle voice answered not Aunt Phoebe —*Julie, this is the best time to practice asking for help. Make some calls and see who can help you this week with the kids.*

I opened up the calendar and grabbed my phone. I was determined to plan the week while giving the kids a winter break of fun. My mom was free to come over in the morning two of the five days. My aunt and uncle were thrilled to come over early to take the kids to breakfast and Beaver Lake Nature Center for a hike. My mother-in-law, Cathy, was available to help as well.

I was so grateful I had people in my life who were early risers.

They agreed to be here around 7 a.m. I drove Jeff to his first chemotherapy treatment with the kids starting their winter break with my mom. I was delighted I didn't need to bring them on the ride. It was enough they would need to come with me to pick Jeff up after his treatment. I was also sad that this was happening. I could be both I suppose…delighted and sad. This mix of opposite emotions I was beginning to accept.

I made prior commitments that I felt I needed to back out of and races I needed to defer to next year. I would say "no" to anything new that came up. My focus needed to be on my family and moving through this challenge. It was ironic because the words I chose for 2022 were connection, community, and courage. How was I going to connect and build community with this 'C' word now in the picture? It didn't look at all how I imagined it. Yet maybe this was exactly how it was supposed to look. I sure did need a lot of courage. Courage in my parenting, courage in my marriage, and courage to face myself. I was facing a mountain. I prayed I had what it took. *God is with me.* This reminder was my anchor. *He is always with me.*

* * *

When Jeff got home after his first treatment he went right to bed and slept for two hours. When he woke he had terrible nausea. I was prepared for him to get sick but he handled his symptoms well. He was instructed by the doctor if this happened to take the nausea medication right away. He did as instructed and it worked like a charm. He went back to bed. I was relieved.

While Jeff slept, I took the kids outside to play. I was doing my best to keep the house quiet. I was happy there was snow on the ground.

"Let's make a snowman." I pulled on my snow pants.

Brindsley and Delaney smiled, "Okay." They did the same. We bundled up and headed outside.

As we rolled the first snowball they asked, "Why is Dad sleeping?"

"The treatment Dad is having will make him very tired. He will be sleeping a lot."

They nodded as they continued rolling their snowball across the lawn. I watched them working together and laughing. I was praying I would know what to say when their questions continued. There was no manual I could refer to yet I could read other people's stories to gain wisdom, strength, and courage.

I don't think it was a coincidence when I joined Writing In Community (WIC) and met Terri Tomoff. I read her book *The Focused Fight: A Childhood Cancer Journey: From Mayhem to Miracles* in 2021, just a few months before learning of my husband's cancer diagnosis. Her family's story gave me hope and courage as my family now faced the dreaded 'C' word.

She writes in her book to look for the nuggets of joy and to manufacture your own sunshine. I took her words to heart as we confronted what the next year would bring. I was determined to not let my fear and anxiety rule over our house. *Manufacturing my sunshine is a blessing I accept.*

I would pray each day— *Please Lord, give me patience, strength, and courage in the months ahead. Open my eyes to your joy, peace, and love as we face this challenge. Help me learn how to dance with uncertainty.*

On the second night of chemotherapy treatment, Jeff didn't sleep well. He woke up several times with night sweats and weird dreams. I tried to sleep but had a hard time. I heard him get up and use the bathroom. I listened for him to flush the toilet twice. I wondered did he close the lid? I didn't hear either. *Oh Julie, stop being such a worry wart.* I would flush the toilet and close the lid when I got up in the morning.

I cleaned the bathroom thoroughly the next day. I got rid of the toothpaste that was dried all over the walls. *What were the kids doing, making artwork with toothpaste?* I had no idea. I changed the sheets so Jeff would have clean ones to sleep in. With the night sweats, I figured it was the best thing to do.

I was happy the kids were playing together well so I could get some cleaning done. By the third day, Jeff was exhausted but he was handling it well. He was eating better and was able to get up to have dinner with us. He mentioned he wasn't sleeping great but the nurse told him it was probably because of the steroid they were giving him before chemotherapy. This made him feel better knowing there was a reason.

* * *

I could hear the rain as my alarm went off. I lay in bed contemplating going for a run or going back to sleep. I recalled the day and decided I better run now, there would be no time later. Jeff had another round of chemotherapy treatment and the kids were home on winter break. *I will get up now and run—it will help me prepare for the day ahead. It will allow me to show up pleasant for my children.*

I repeated— *Get out the door and I will feel better. Lace-up my sneakers and find my inner playmate.*

I slipped my clothes on which I laid out the night before. I laced up my sneakers and stepped outside. The rain had let up. My stride amplified over the damp road. It felt like spring— my feet the birdsong.

The wind lifted my ponytail. The cool breeze kissed my face. Comfort, peace, and encouragement filled my bones. *We are going to get through this.* I was alert to the roar and whoosh of the streams as I ran past. Water splashed up with each stride as I made my way to the village. The sound of the stream loosened the tension in my shoulders and face. My eyebrows clenched now relaxed.

The roads or trails were my place of refuge. My runs allowed me space to process my fear, sadness, and anger. We were on day three of Jeff's chemotherapy and running was my outlet. I was grateful to be outdoors— nature could handle my big emotions.

My focus turned to the stream, the earthy smell, and my breath. The niggles in my right hip, calf, and foot softened with each bound. I smiled. I felt peace and joy. I was manufacturing my sunshine with each stride.

I thanked my mind and body for working together. I repeated the mantra—*One day at a time. One step at a time.*

It's Your Move:

Farmer Carry March and Geese

Check out the It's Your Move channel: www.youtube.com/@juliebhughes

CHAPTER 21

FUN FRIDAY

On day four of chemotherapy, Jeff was doing better than I imagined. By now, I thought I would be up all night cleaning vomit and changing the sheets but thankfully my imagination was wildly incorrect.

He was waking up in the middle of the night but not to get sick. He was waking up drenched in sweat. I would hear the opening and closing of his dresser drawers. I would sit up in bed to see him stripping off his soaked shirt to grab a new, dry one. "Do you need help?" I recall whispering to him in the dark and realizing how silly I sounded. He was a grown man, of course, he could put on a shirt.

Luckily, he didn't say anything mean, just "No thank you, I'm fine" as he walked back over to the bed. Jeff was so patient with me. I found myself not knowing what to do. This expectation I had on myself to constantly be doing something, I needed to let go of. Jeff would tell me if he needed me. He would ask. I didn't want to nag him or bother him. I wanted to give him space and not suffocate him with constant questions.

I was happy I shared this in one of my writing sessions. My friend Terri chimed in with the best idea. "Place a stack of shirts next to the bed so he can just reach down and grab one."

Why didn't I think of that? It was so helpful. I appreciated Terri sharing this information with me. She knew all too well as her son was a five-time cancer survivor. He too experienced night sweats.

* * *

Jeff was very tired. His stomach was off and he was not feeling great. Which was to be expected. These drugs were strong and not healthy for his body or mind. Yet this poison was being given to him to kill the cancer cells.

Does this even make sense? This is what we do to treat cancer.

I guess I never thought about it until now. Yet what was the choice? Toxic drugs or death? Give him the cocktail of drugs and it better work.

I was so mad. I was sad for his body having to have this crap in every cell, every tissue. Yet I had to accept this was the best option. We were doing the right thing.

* * *

"Fun Friday!" I shouted to Brindsley and Delaney. Winter break was coming to an end. I was determined to end the week with some fun. I wondered if I had let them down. They were sitting on the floor playing in the living room. I loved how they made up games with their stuffed animals.

My mom was on the couch waiting for me to get home. I just returned from dropping Jeff off at his last chemotherapy treatment for the week. I was eager to take the kids sledding. We had a great deal of snow on the ground and I knew the perfect place— the library.

It had the best hill. We would grab some books after to warm up. We got our snow gear on, grabbed our sleds, and headed to the library.

Brindsley dashed to the top with his sled and off he went. Delaney and I squeezed into a sled together and zoomed down. The snow flew up into our faces as we raced down the hill. Delaney squealed with delight and I laughed. I forgot how much fun sledding was.

It felt good to laugh but Aunt Phoebe chimed in with her squeaky voice, "How can you be happy when your husband has cancer? How can you be having fun when Jeff is sitting by himself getting poison dripped into his arm?"

GRR. This was my battle. *Can I be happy when Jeff is sick? Can I have fun and enjoy life even during this challenge?*

This was a struggle for me. I was glad my children allowed me to notice. I was happy to be aware of these thoughts. I wanted to show them we could still find joy even during the dark times. We didn't have to mope around or deprive ourselves of the goodness and beauty in life.

Brindsley hopped on the sled with me next and we laughed down the hill. He rolled off the sled to stop and make a snow angel. I did the same. Several times, Brindsley would stop during sledding and hug me. My heart was full.

We stopped at the library next for some books and then to Skytop, a local coffee shop for hot chocolate and a cookie. I was happy I had the energy to show up for them today.

Even though we were going through this awful thing, our children were handling it well, at least today they were. They were kids without a care in the world. The thought of Dad being sick was off their minds at this moment. I couldn't have asked for a better day. Laughing and playing with them was a joy. I hoped these were the memories they would remember out of this season.

* * *

I was tired. I worked hard to rally. Jeff was up a lot going to the bathroom. It would wake me every time. *Does he need me?* The interrupted sleep was difficult. I could feel it in my body. My right hip would sting. My right heel had a sharp pain without any warning. I had these symptoms before. My nervous system was looking out for me, my harm alarm dialed up. My lack of sleep, Jeff's condition, financial concerns, and extra responsibility all contributed to my discomfort. I would remind myself, *this pain does not mean harm.*

Jeff slept most days and felt weak and off. He was disappointed. He thought he would feel better. This was the hard part. *Why would he have this expectation?* I was confused. He just started chemotherapy. We had a ways to go. Yet I didn't say anything. What would that accomplish?

I got busy with the chores while Jeff slept on the couch. This was where he was stationed most of the day. At least he was by a window, to look out of when he felt like it. I could cook, clean, take care of the kids, and meet their needs but I felt I couldn't meet his. I could make the bed so he had clean sheets to sleep in, wash his clothes, and make dinner…but I couldn't take away his pain, grief, or disappointment. *It is frustrating to see a loved one hurting, to see a loved one sick. One day at a time…*

I repeated—*one day at a time*— in hopes it would keep me focused and grounded during this season of trouble. To keep steady and be a rock for my family. I would keep moving, running, and writing. Sleep and nutrition would be a priority. I would stick to my bedtime routine as best I could. I was determined to stay healthy to care for my family.

It's Your Move:
Seated Nerve Flossing
Check out the It's Your Move channel: www.youtube.com/@juliebhughes

CHAPTER 22

WRESTLE WITH HURT

He punched his small fists
into his pillow—
My heart broke open
as I watched my son
wrestle with hurt
and anger.
And all I could do was
hold him.
And all I could
do was listen to his pain.
And all I could do was
be present
And remind him
that what he was feeling
was okay.

Brindsley shouts "Cancer is ruining 2022!"

Yes, it was. I wasn't going to argue his statement. I kept silent. This year was not what we had planned or expected. I couldn't believe it came back after ten years.

Brindsley ran into his room and I followed. He punched his bed, then his pillow. I felt like it was my gut. My stomach clenched with distress.

"Dad is always sleeping now, he can't put me to bed. He won't even play with me."

My heart hurt. My body crumbled to the bed. I sat next to him and placed my arm around him, holding him tight. I felt every word he said yet didn't know what to do or say other than hold him and agree— It was ruining 2022.

I was grateful he was sharing how he felt rather than holding it in. I didn't want him to carry this burden alone. I was relieved he felt safe and secure to shout out his frustration, pain, anger, and disappointment. I see him. I hear his pain. He was not alone. I made sure to validate his feelings and remind him we were in this together. It was temporary and we would be okay and stronger because of this.

We hugged each other. "We love you so much Brindsley. We are going to get through this."

* * *

Let's go for a drive
The destination
up in the air—
What joy lies around the bend?
I'm determined
to find it.

I walked in from a run and pulled off my gloves and hat. There was Jeff, just where he was an hour ago slumped on the couch with blankets bundled around him. His face turned toward the window. He did not look good.

My heart felt sick. I wanted to take all my happy hormones from my run and give them to him. I hated he had to endure this and a part of me wished it was me instead of him.

What can I do? I searched my brain for something to cheer him up…a drive.

I walked over to him and placed my hand on his shoulder, "Let's go."

He looked at me and shrugged.

"Come on, let's go for a drive it will be good to get you out of the house."

I was happy he didn't resist the idea and agreed. I had no idea where we would drive but trusted I would know once I got into the car. I made a quick change of my clothes before he changed his mind. He bundled up and grabbed a hat.

Cazenovia was a small village about 15 minutes away. We hadn't been there in a while so I headed in that direction. I turned the music on thinking maybe that would help his mood.

We parked the car and sat for a minute —now what? I wasn't sure if he would feel like walking. Jeff was tired. His stamina wasn't great which was to be expected with the chemotherapy treatments he had endured so far. He unbuckled his seatbelt and said, "Let's walk a bit."

I smiled, "Alright."

I was happy he was willing to give it a go. We checked out the local shops for a few minutes on foot then headed back to the car. He was cold. I suggested we find a coffee shop to warm up. We buckled up and headed to Toast, a local coffee/bakery shop down the road.

We stepped into the shop. My nose inhaled sweet bread, muffins, and cookies. I looked at Jeff as he smiled at the choices under the clean, window displays. "Jules, look at these cookies!" He was thrilled.

I was delighted to see the shift in his mood over cookies. I was so happy—Jeff was back. His entire posture changed and for a moment I forgot he was sick. I forgot all about next week's round of chemotherapy. My friend Terri Tomoff was right— "Don't underestimate the power of a chocolate chip cookie" and I will add to that— and a drive… just for the 'fun' of it.

It's Your Move:
Hip Airplane
Check out the It's Your Move channel: www.youtube.com/@juliebhughes

CHAPTER 23

EVEN THOUGH

To run in nature
unbroken state of surprise.
Stick around—
something is bound
to happen…

I felt my energy, creativity, and my love for running growing faint. The last few days I'd struggled with getting out the door to run and sitting down to write. I'd managed to do a little of both but it took all the energy in me to lace up my sneakers and to pick up the pen.

Jeff and the kids required my support, encouragement, and help…it was hard to find anything left for me. *I write this and feel guilt, loss, sadness, defeat, and anger. I'm sure there are many other emotions inside of me.* Could I sit and feel them all?

I'm telling myself I can. I can handle any emotion that comes up. I want to believe this.

One day at a time. It was true this season. I had my intentions set— I would write and run today, and yet…I needed to allow myself to adapt and pivot. I would listen to my body. Somedays that meant I needed more rest. It was okay to take a nap. It was okay to sleep in and run later. Somedays that meant reading a book instead of doing the dishes or cleaning the house. It was okay if the bathrooms weren't spotless.

I was allowed to give myself grace. I missed my early morning runs before the kids were up. I missed the darkness and solitude. My ritual. Yet my body was asking for more sleep. I trusted that this new routine of running later would work just fine. *It's okay to change things up. Yes, it looks different and this too shall pass. Julie, keep showing up.*

* * *

I recall one weekend run. I was slow and a few strides behind Felicia, my Saturday run buddy. I didn't have the energy to keep up during some parts of the run. I was beginning to beat myself up. I apologized as I pushed to catch up to her. She was not bothered one bit. She kept her pace and continued to encourage me as I focused on her words pulling me along instead of my worries.

She looked over her left shoulder, "Today's run is about conversation, movement, and being in nature, that's what we are doing right now. Don't worry about pace, speed, or time—just run for enjoyment."

I was grateful for her kind words. It was just what I needed to hear to quiet my inner judge. My focus returned to the sights, sounds, and smells of nature.

I noticed two bluebirds and a cardinal. I heard a downy woodpecker drum from above. The sunrise covered the sky in bright pink as we made our way uphill. I inhaled the smell of pine needles. The tension in my face and shoulders relaxed. The grip of my fists released. I took some deep breaths and smiled to myself. What a gorgeous morning.

I was so thankful I had Felicia running ahead of me to keep me going. I didn't want to get out of bed but I was happy I showed up to see this beautiful sunrise. It energized me. It gave me peace and filled me with hope.

Even though my pace was slow. Even though I was worried I was slowing Felicia down. Even though Jeff was suffering through chemotherapy treatments. Even though I was scared, anxious, and full of doubt. *I will rejoice and be glad. I will rejoice and be glad.*

When I came home from my run Delaney was playing a game, "I'm the doctor and you're the patients."

She was talking to me and Brindsley while she sat at her desk. In a very serious tone, she looked at me, "Mom what's your problem."

I replied, "I'm tired" as I plopped onto her bed.

She nods, "Okay you have chemo."

I tried not to laugh. "No Delaney, I'm just tired."

She stood up from her desk with her hands on her hips, "Mom that's not a problem."

"Okay, my legs are tired."

That seemed to satisfy her as she instructed me to lie down on the bed while she examined my legs.

Oh good, I can rest my eyes for a bit. I loved these kinds of games.

Delaney gently rubbed the back of my lower leg for what seemed like a few hours. I closed my eyes trying to squeeze in a cat nap.

She announced, "All better, you are free to go."

I opened my eyes and smiled, "Thank you, Delaney. I do feel so much better."

I rested on her bed for a few minutes listening to my children play doctor. My heart was sad and happy. I was filled with both emotions. I allowed myself to sit with them.

I can be happy and sad.

It's Your Move:
Split Stance Heel Raise
Check out the It's Your Move channel: www.youtube.com/@juliebhughes

CHAPTER 24

SEVENTEEN AND THE WIG

I got up at 5 a.m. and ran seven miles. Praise the Lord! I felt so happy to be outside in the dark cold morning. The roads were clear and dry. The neighborhood was quiet—just my strides on the road and my breath. I found myself planning out the loop in my head. This would get me at least an hour of running and I would be home before anyone was up.

I made my climb uphill, then took a right down a small incline. My legs were grateful for a break. It was just what I needed and happy for it. My pace picked up and my discomfort softened a bit. My right hip had been more noticeable these last several weeks. I was aware of my nervous system protecting me, perhaps watching out for any more danger. I know the nerves detect not just physical danger, injury, or sickness, but also my thoughts, stress, and emotions. I acknowledged what we were going through wasn't easy. We were all doing the best we could with the circumstances.

Jeff was still sleeping. He had a tough time at night getting comfortable. Night sweats, headaches, or the use of the bathroom had been waking him up. I would hear the toilet flush or the rustling of him changing his clothes. I felt bad there was nothing I could do. I woke up to ask if he needed anything from me but he didn't. We were not sure why the night sweats kept coming but they did…one of the many side effects.

Seventeen had been the number in the back of my mind. The day that Jeff's hair may start to fall out from what we'd been told. He said his scalp had been feeling funny and very sensitive the last two days. He took off his shirt and noticed the discomfort as it grazed his head.

I recall when she mentioned this number at chemo teach. "Day seventeen you will learn if your hair will stay or go." I sat across from her thinking, maybe he would be the patient who didn't lose his hair. It looked so full and thick. I couldn't believe all his hair would fall out. It seemed impossible.

We told Brindsley and Delaney that Dad would probably lose his hair. We thought it would be best to prepare them. I wondered what the reaction would be when they saw their Dad bald and with no facial hair. To be honest, I wondered what my reaction would be.

Jeff always had thick hair with either a beard, mustache, or both. I tried to imagine him without any hair. I visualized each day for a moment. I know that might sound strange but it was my way to prepare myself. I didn't want to freak out or be shocked in front of the kids so I did my best to imagine him without any hair.

When day seventeen arrived they were right— Jeff's hair started falling out in chunks. He started to laugh as he pulled out the grey hairs at the side of his head.

"Hey, maybe I'll just lose the greys but keep everything else." I loved his sense of humor shining through this terrible situation. We both smiled.

The next day Jeff noticed some of his hair on his pillow when he woke up. He ran his fingers through his hair and a clump fell into his hand. He showed it to me and declared, "I'll wait and see maybe I won't lose my hair."

As the day went on more hair was found on the couch, on his clothes, and in his hands as he ran his fingers through his hair. He turned to me with a calm voice, "I'm going to get my hair buzzed off tomorrow."

The next day he woke up to more clumps of hair on his pillow. He went into the shower and looked down to find clumps of hair next to the shower drain.

He announced, "I'm going down the road to get my head shaved. I don't want my hair to clog up the pipes."

I nodded. I tried to keep myself from laughing, clogging the drain was the least of my worries.

"Okay, do you want me to go with you?" I hoped he would say yes.

He replied, "No, I want to go alone."

I respected his decision. I could tell it was bothering him that his hair was falling out. He would rather not watch it happen clump after clump.

While he was gone, I gathered all the hats I could find and placed them in a pile. It was still very cold here in Syracuse, New York, and Jeff always had so much hair, a beard, and a mustache. He recalled only one time in high school when he got a buzz cut from a friend, other than that he has had a lot of hair his entire adult life. When we got married it was rather long, to the lower part of his neck and past his ears. He enjoyed his hair.

We told the kids that Dad would be without hair when they got home from school. Jeff explained that the treatment was causing his hair to fall out.

Brindsley inquired, "Will it grow back?"

Jeff answered, "Oh yes it will grow back, it might just take a while."

Delaney then looked at Jeff, "You can wear my Elsa wig, Dad." We all laughed.

I was so happy Brindsley and Delaney were asking questions. It gave me reassurance they felt safe and like they say, "Knowledge is power." I was hopeful the knowledge they were seeking was helping them positively cope with this circumstance.

Jeff was happy to discover he did not have a pointed head or any strange markings with his hair completely gone. We laughed. His head was perfectly round and he wore "no hair" very well. He was pleased with the change and seemed to be taking it all in stride.

"Hey, I don't have to do my hair anymore. That's a pretty good deal." His hair would grow back and among the many side effects of chemotherapy seemed to be the easiest to accept.

* * *

I recall one morning, Jeff sat at the kitchen table. He was slumped over his bald head resting on his hand. He didn't feel well. He was on round two of chemotherapy.

Delaney came out from her bedroom and looked at Jeff for a moment. She asked if she could touch his head. She patted her small hand on his head as Jeff grinned. His head was perfect—evenly round.

He laughed, "I look good bald!"

He truly did.

I loved that Jeff could laugh. He found joy even when he felt awful, tired, and weak.

He then commented on how his head was cold.

I chimed in, "I'll buy some more hats for you." I was thrilled there was something I could do. Jeff joked about shopping for wigs and that's when Delaney disappeared from the kitchen.

She came back carrying her long white-haired wig. It was part of her costume when she dressed up as Elyse from the movie Frozen. She handed it to Jeff. He examined it for a moment as we waited to see what he would do.

He placed it over his head and smiled.

Delaney shouted, "Brindsley come look at Dad!"

Brindsley came out from his room to see what the commotion was.

Delaney's eyes widened as she hugged Jeff. Brindsley did too. I was so happy to see Jeff show up for Delaney when he felt so lousy. He was answering back with joy. We laughed as we stood in the kitchen. Jeff wearing a white-haired wig and a grin from ear to ear.

We are going to be okay.

It's Your Move:
Squeeze Shoulder Blades and Roll It Out
Check out the It's Your Move channel: www.youtube.com/@juliebhughes

CHAPTER 25

JOY IN A BASKET

Joy in a basket
Openness to receive love
I can learn this too

Did you know they made lollipops for nausea? Oncology skin care and lip balm? I was clueless. My friends were not. In the weeks leading up to Jeff's first chemotherapy treatment, my friend Stacey was rallying the troops. She gathered several of my friends to chip in to support Jeff and our family.

She showed up at our front door with a large basket in her arms full of items. I was not expecting this. I was just grateful to see her. I needed a hug.

She walked in with her contagious smile. A bounce in her step. She handed me the basket and Jeff stood up from the couch to greet her. Brindsley and Delaney came running in curious to see who was at the door. They were thrilled to know there was something for them. My friends thought of everything.

Peppermint tea, throat drops, and word searches to give Jeff something to do during chemotherapy treatments. A gift card for me for coffee and games for the kids. She must have spent hours ordering everything. Yellow sticky notes were placed on each item to relay to Jeff the benefit. *Who does this?* Our kind, generous friend Stacey does. I hugged her again and whispered thank you over and over. *What else do I say? What else do I do?*

I was learning to receive and that was enough. *I can learn this.*

Jeff found every item in the basket helpful as his treatment started. The lollipops were a blessing for him to consume when he was feeling yucky or when he didn't feel like eating. I hadn't thought about things like this. What a blessing I had friends step up to think for me. It was joy in a basket.

My mom and Jeff's parents brought over meals and watched the children so I could take Jeff to his appointments. They gave me the necessary breaks from driving and were willing to step in when and where they could.

Our neighbor walked over one afternoon carrying something in his hands. Jeff and I were sitting outside to enjoy the sun. It was a welcome sight from the gloomy, grey days. He handed Jeff two winter beanie hats with knitted beards attached. I had no idea these existed. Jeff put one on and was happy to have a beard back to warm his face.

It was a wonderful, kind gesture and it gave us a laugh. I couldn't wait for Brindsley and Delaney to get home so we could show them. Our neighbor made our day.

This is why we need others. We need community. I didn't have the energy or capacity to shop for these items or even think about these items. I was so grateful to have friends who did. Friends who showed up even when they could have chosen not to.

I learned that sharing the difficulties of the day or the struggle I was experiencing with friends or family helped release some of the big emotions I was holding. They were willing to help me carry the load just by listening. I appreciated those I could be vulnerable with—it took courage. I realize how blessed I was to have others meet me with love, kindness, and courage. To truly be interested in how we were doing. They showed up in ways I wasn't expecting and this kindness fueled my days. *One step at a time.*

* * *

My sister-in-law called from Rochester, NY, "Text me your order from Wegmans and we will have it delivered to your home." My friend, Carrie-Anne in Pottstown, PA, sent me a text, "What do you want from Olive Garden or Carrabas? We will get it delivered to you."

I hesitated for a moment speechless at their thoughtfulness. Dumbfounded as I stared at my phone. *They can provide us with a meal in another town or city…*distance would not stand in their way. Family and friends came alongside us even though we were miles apart. I didn't expect this.

My view of what I thought community meant changed. It doesn't require folks living in the same geographical location. Connection, kindness, encouragement, and like-minded people had no boundaries.

Members of the church we attended at the time kindly brought our family a meal once a week for two months to help us out. Each week, a different person would park in our driveway and deliver a warm, home-cooked meal for us to enjoy. My children loved the fun surprise of seeing who would show up with food each time. It brought them joy and something to look forward to each week. I was glad I accepted the church's offer since initially, I was going to turn it down.

The thought, *I can handle meals— I'm not sick* surfaced.

I was happy I accepted their offer and allowed their gifts of food in our home. Seeing the joy on my children's faces as they peeked inside the grocery bags to see what dinner would be that night showed me the positive impact. If I had declined the offer, I wouldn't have realized how my old view of avoiding reliance on others was not serving me or my family. These meals were a true blessing during this difficult time.

It allowed me the chance to teach my children. To be a role model to them— to show them how to receive and how to give. We needed to learn how to be open to both grace and gratitude. What a beautiful lesson I learned during this difficult season. What a gift.

It's Your Move:
Side Plank (Modified and Full)
Check out the It's Your Move channel: www.youtube.com/@juliebhughes

CHAPTER 26

STRESSFUL PIVOT

Jeff's treatment times varied each day. Some started at 7:30 a.m. some at 8:00. They were about six hours long. He would bring reading material, podcasts to listen to, and word puzzles to keep him busy. He packed himself some snacks and a small lunch in case he got hungry. I wasn't allowed to sit with him during treatment. Since COVID-19 the rules had changed— no one else was allowed to sit with their loved one during chemotherapy.

Each morning I would pull up to the entrance of the clinic to drop Jeff off. He would lean in for a kiss and hug before he got out. I felt awful I couldn't go with him. I felt sick as I watched him enter the clinic by himself with his bag of goodies hung over his shoulder.

It just didn't seem right he had to sit there alone. I was angry. I was sad.

In my mind, I pictured myself there keeping him company. We would play cards, do crossword puzzles together, and talk sports. I would tell him about the kids and what they were up to. I would make sure he ate something and drank lots of water. I would help him to the bathroom if he were feeling weak or nauseated.

I was confident he was being cared for by an amazing team of clinicians yet as his wife I felt this duty to be there. My expectations would not be met as Jeff disappeared into the clinic and I drove home.

Yet maybe it was better this way. I could run, get groceries, clean the house, make meals, and accomplish whatever else came up. I would take action and embrace the circumstance instead of resisting it.

Each round of chemotherapy was 21 days. Jeff had treatment for five days in a row with a break on the weekend. He would then return to the clinic on Monday for the hardest treatment of the cycle. He had the rest of the week off and then would return for one more short treatment on Monday. It was after this treatment he would be given a medicine called Neulasta. It was a device the nurse placed on the skin of his upper arm. It would self-inject the medicine the next day and the dose would take 45 minutes to complete. He would then remove the device once the status light was solid green.

He was informed of the side effects— bone pain and feeling pretty miserable. Fun. He was not looking forward to experiencing this each cycle. Yet the reason for it was to prevent him from getting sick, or an infection, and keep him out of the hospital during his treatments. The chemotherapy caused the white blood cells to drop and having this after each round kept them from dropping more.

After each round of chemotherapy, Jeff had a check-in with Dr. Duffy to monitor his symptoms and check his blood work. He had a separate appointment to monitor his lung function. This was the new routine after each 21-day cycle.

We were really happy with the care we were receiving and how attentive Dr. Duffy and his staff were. He asked questions, listened well, and stayed on top of Jeff's care by reaching out to other oncologists. I appreciated he was willing to collaborate with others. He treated us like family and so did the staff. Their office operated in a kind and caring way. They were the 'care' in healthcare. We were in good hands and kept the faith his cancer would be zero by the end of the four cycles, by the end of May 2022.

At Jeff's first check-in after round one of chemotherapy, we were concerned about his hearing. His tinnitus had increased significantly and he noticed he could no longer hear the beep of the coffee maker when brewed. Dr. Duffy was concerned. He recommended his hearing be checked to get a baseline. It would be a guide to see if there was more decline as chemotherapy treatment continued.

Dr. Duffy did mention he could switch out the drug that was the culprit of the hearing loss however the evidence showed taking this drug away decreased the chances for a cure. Jeff didn't want to change the plan. He agreed to continue with the cocktail of drugs understanding his hearing loss may be irreversible. Jeff would take his chances even though hearing aids may be in his future.

Jeff agreed to call an audiologist. He had a hearing test done at the end of the week and it showed some loss. We weren't sure yet if it would return, get worse, or stay the same after the chemotherapy. Time would tell and we would cross that bridge when we needed to.

In the meantime, we would be proactive and monitor his hearing after every cycle of treatment. I encouraged him to eat bananas. They were loaded with magnesium and potassium both important to hearing well. I had hope in the mighty banana and a bowl of this fruit would be found in our kitchen in case Jeff wanted one.

I realize how ridiculous I may have sounded...was a banana any match for these drugs?

It's Your Move:
Grab Your Sword
Check out the It's Your Move channel: www.youtube.com/@juliebhughes

CHAPTER 27

EXPECTATIONS OF A CAREGIVER

I got out of bed at 5:15 a.m. for a run. I was happy I had the energy as we headed into round two of Jeff's treatments. I was showing up but just felt slow. I was training to run the Syracuse Half Marathon which was in five days. I was back and forth on whether I would toe the start line. I wanted to see how Jeff felt over the weekend before I decided. I didn't want to leave him home alone if he wasn't feeling well.

On my run, I saw an orange moon. It was breathtaking. I felt this new flow of energy as I ran. The moon guiding me step by step. I was grateful I was up to enjoy this gift — something to write about when I got home.

I slipped in the door. When I sat down to write I noticed a card on the table. Jeff must have placed it there the night before. It was a handwritten note from him. It made my day. What a surprise.

I felt seen. I felt appreciated. Both of which I felt low on since his health challenge began. It made me smile— more fuel for my day.

I made a pot of coffee and then went to wake up my mom. She spent the night so she could stay with the kids while I dropped Jeff off. He had another early appointment. I didn't want to bring the kids. I wanted them to be able to sleep and get ready for school at their normal time. I was happy my mom was available. I was doing my best to keep the kid's routine the same. I figured this would benefit them while we navigated this challenge.

During round two, Jeff slept most of the day and didn't see the kids much. His appetite was absent. He mentioned his taste was off, even the hot sauce was bland. This made him frustrated and down.

"I hope it comes back, it's so hard to want to eat."

He tasted a metallic taste when drinking water. Could you imagine? It was something they told us would happen. It was something he was waiting for but hoped it wouldn't come. I could tell when he sat at the table with us he didn't want to eat. He was trying to force himself to take a bite of something however his forehead rested in his hands most of the time. He was exhausted.

The doctor was adamant about his weight. He didn't want him getting lower than 150 pounds. Jeff was hovering at this number for a few days now. I was starting to worry his next weight check would be under the number. If this happened he might need to be admitted to the hospital. We were trying so hard to keep him home during his treatment.

I didn't know what to do to encourage him to eat or drink. I looked across the table with a feeling of helplessness. Something I'd felt since this challenge began. It was persistent. I was stressed thinking about how much weight he had lost. I blamed myself for not knowing what would taste good. If I could just make the right meal, his weight wouldn't be a problem. *I know, I know, my wicked mind.*

How do I sit with this emotion and not let it get the best of me?

Surrender.

It dawned on me. At that moment, I wasn't here to fix Jeff. It wasn't my job to fight what I had no control over. What occurred to me was— *I'm just here to love him in this difficult circumstance.* This realization freed me from the expectations I was placing on myself as a caregiver.

I was willing to recognize nobody was better at running our lives than the One whose ways were higher than our own. *God will see us through.*

* * *

I found myself asking—What else can I do to bring my husband joy, comfort, or strength? What else besides a hug, a kiss, or a smile? What else besides a meal, a note of encouragement, or a smoothie? What else besides another blanket or heat pad?

What else can I do?

I wonder if other caregivers find themselves asking this question.

I caught myself when "How do you feel?" wanted to slip out. I made a point not to ask. I felt that wouldn't be a helpful question. I would get frustrated with hearing that over and over. *I feel like crap…I have cancer what do you think!*

I learned to ask better questions. *How can I help you get more comfortable? Would you like me to get you a drink or any medication? Would you like me to take you for a drive? Do you feel up for a short walk?*

I learned to trust that he would tell me. I got better at sitting still, holding my tongue, and being available when he needed me. It wasn't easy. Aunt Phoebe would squeak in with her bossy tone…you have things to do, you can't sit around, and look at all the chores to be done. *Sigh.*

I paid attention to my reactions and thoughts. I learned not to listen to Aunt Phoebe. I noticed sitting with Jeff and not saying a word was what he needed the most.

One of the many books I read during this time was called, Fight Back with Joy: Celebrate More. Regret Less. Stare Down Your Greatest Fears. by Margaret Feinberg. She shared her cancer journey and how she fought back with joy. It helped to get her point of view as the patient. I loved her determination and focus on choosing joy. Here she was undergoing treatment and her courage to take action despite her circumstances was inspiring. I wanted to do this for my family.

Where do I find joy? How can I fight back with joy?

She wrote some examples of what she did. I was on board with doing the same. This was what I decided— buy balloons to celebrate after each round of chemotherapy, write encouraging notes to Jeff and the children, make special treats, and find joy in the simple, everyday moments.

I was reminded of the beauty in each day as I ran. I found joy from an encouraging letter in the mail or a text message from a friend, the hugs from my children, the laughter in playing games or rolling in the snow. The joy of just being together with Jeff on the couch as we read stories.

She was right— there truly was so much to be joyful for.

It's Your Move:

Bridge With March

Check out the It's Your Move channel: www.youtube.com/@juliebhughes

Chapter 28

TEACHABLE SPIRIT

The Syracuse Half-Marathon was my first race of 2022. Speedwork, fartlek workouts, and negative split training runs were all necessary for me to run faster. However, this training didn't happen over the last several months so I took the pressure off on time or pace.

I was confident my husband would give anything to be at this race cheering me on. Instead, he was on the couch battling nausea, tinnitus, and fatigue, the side effects he was experiencing at the time. I felt helpless. There wasn't anything I could do but sit with him. My hesitation to leave and race consumed me. *Should I still go? Should I leave him here by himself? Should I even think about racing at a time like this?* The should-ing on myself was not helping.

The guilt overwhelmed me. The belief that I needed to be around 24/7 or things would fall apart, weighed on my mind. This was a lie. Running and racing were actions I enjoyed for self-care. Even though the guilt was present, I stuck with my plan to toe the start line.

It felt great to be back at a race with a crowd of runners huddled together. The rain decided to hold off as we waited for the start. We were racing 13.1 miles through the streets of Syracuse, New York. The goal for me on this race day: *talk kind to myself and appreciate I get to run.*

BANG! We were off. The beat of our sneakers drummed the road ahead. Smiles, laughter, shouts, and cheers filled the streets. I recalled my goals to myself as runners passed me up the hill— *have fun, talk kind to myself, and finish.*

At mile nine, when my thighs ached, and the back of my legs burned, I thought about

Jeff and what he was going through. I shook out my arms. My eyes fixed on a group of runners ahead of me. *I can do this. Run strong for Jeff. Keep looking up. Keep going.* My goal was to keep the pack of runners in sight and not back down. I continued these mantras until I saw the finish line.

I wore my watch but didn't bother to start it. I was not here to get a personal record. I raced to show my children that even in the hard parts of life we must keep going.

I looked ahead to the finish. Thrilled I was almost there. When I crossed the line I was met by my high school cross-country coach Jim Paccia. He placed a medal around my neck and then gave me a big hug— "Congratulations, Julie." It was great to see a familiar face at the finish. I missed the kids and Jeff waiting for me at the end.

Overall, I was happy with my performance. I brought a good attitude, encouraged myself, had fun, and I finished. Even though my training wasn't how I expected—I showed up. It was a great confidence booster. I couldn't wait to get home and share my morning with Jeff and the kids. The medal was always a highlight for Brindsley and Delaney. *Who will try on the bling first?*

* * *

I got home and put my feet up to rest. I wondered what I had in the refrigerator to make for dinner. *Do we need to eat again?* I closed my eyes hoping that would help my thinking when I heard the doorbell. I wondered who it could be.

Brindsley and Delaney were playing together and Jeff was on the couch in and out of sleep. I got up and went to the door but no one was there when I opened it. I saw my friend heading to her car. She turned around, "I don't want to bother you but I dropped off some food."

I was so surprised. What timing? How did she know I was just thinking about dinner? I had nothing prepared. My failure turned into a beautiful gift from my friend. I waved and thanked her as she pulled out of our driveway. I looked down. Sitting outside by the front door was a bag with two square aluminum tins. One was homemade macaroni and cheese and the other a dessert.

Generosity was a gift I was learning to receive without guilt.

I was learning to accept these gifts of love and hope without obligation. I was letting go of the idea I needed to give or do something in return. This was not easy yet this season was teaching me. *I will have a teachable spirit.*

It's Your Move:

March or Walk With Upper Arm Movements

Check out the It's Your Move channel: www.youtube.com/@juliebhughes

CHAPTER 29

MUD OF LIFE

Felicia and I headed to Highland Forest for our long run. We registered to run a 50K ultra at the end of May. We needed practice running over roots, through mud, and navigating the terrain of the trails. On several Saturdays, we would choose Highland Forest in Fabius, New York to prepare instead of the roads.

I questioned my decision. *Do I run an ultra when Jeff is sick?*

I countered back—*Why not? What if this training is helping me stay strong for my family during this challenge?* I held onto this question, repeating to myself when guilt or self-doubt would creep in.

The fresh air, the bright green ferns covered the side of the trail, and the trees protected us from the rain. The course marked out for us was challenging— roots to be mindful of, steep elevations to ascend and descend, streams to cross, and thick patches of mud.

I was happy to keep my balance as I ran through the first mud pit. My feet slid, left and then right with each stride. I laughed with Felicia. I was happy I kept my balance and stayed upright. When we approached the next muddy trail, I decided to look for dry patches of grass or run toward the outer edges instead of running straight through. I didn't want to fall and figured this was a good idea.

My energy was focused on getting around the mud instead of just charging through. I realized how much mental energy I was using to do this. I could feel my legs getting tired as I maneuver around the mud leading to a longer route.

I got this. Keep picking my feet up. This run is gorgeous.

My thoughts kept me going as we made our climb up some steep terrain. We were cruising right along chatting away when my toe caught a root. I didn't pick my foot up enough. I landed face-first in the mud. My knees and palms had a squishing landing, luckily my face stayed out of it. I bounced right back up and wiped my hands off on my pants.

Felicia stopped and turned around, "Are you okay?"

"Oh yes, I'm fine. It didn't hurt at all."

I laughed it off, grateful for the soft landing. My inner playmate roared with laughter and chanted— *Mud is fun! Mud is fun!* I was grateful for the mud and the joy I felt.

It brought back memories of running trails as a kid and mud runs in high school cross-country. We would be covered from head to toe in mud and loved it. I never dodged around the mud. I headed straight for it willing to accept the challenge.

Today I was trying to avoid the mud. Why? I didn't want to fall yet it happened anyway. All my energy was focused on escaping the mud rather than facing it head-on. It reminded me of life. *We can try to go around, ignore, or flee from life's challenges yet what's the payoff?*

Today I was reminded of this. *How will I become stronger, more adaptable, confident, and develop resilience if I avoid the challenges? I won't.*

It's life's challenges that help us grow and discover our capabilities.

And I was discovering it was better with others— to pull you up, dust you off, and cheer you on.

* * *

I recall one Sunday morning when Jeff was having a difficult time getting comfortable. His legs felt heavy and they hurt. The side effects of the Neulesta. I rubbed his thighs for 15 minutes in hopes of giving him some comfort. It was hard to see him like this. I wished there was more I could do for him. He still had one more cycle of chemotherapy to go. He wished he was done. He wanted to feel good again. I wanted this for him too.

I sat with him on the couch for a while. It was hard to be still. I noticed this urgency in me to get things done. The house was a mess. I had piles of laundry to fold and put away. Dishes in the sink and of course the bathrooms. I felt bad that it was hard for me even when Jeff was sick to sit with him. *How can the laundry and cleaning be more important than your husband?* Yikes, that thought was hard to hear.

I believe this time was teaching me to practice being still. I thought I already knew how. The Lord with His great sense of humor— I needed more practice.

Be still with Jeff, the dishes can wait, and the laundry can wait. Just sit with him and be still.

It's okay to rest. It's okay to be still. Courage over comfort.

It's Your Move:
No More Laundry
Check out the It's Your Move channel: www.youtube.com/@juliebhughes

CHAPTER 30

HITTING THE WALL

At the end of the third round, Jeff was struggling.

His side effects were getting the best of him. His hearing had declined. The tinnitus had increased. He was experiencing peripheral neuropathy, pain, tingling, and numbness in his hands and feet. A side effect of the chemotherapy that was very common. He was becoming very sensitive to temperature changes. He noticed his fingers would turn white, and feel cold, and he would have difficulty using his hands. His appetite was off.

He was tired physically and mentally. We were at mile 18 of the marathon, it was how I was dealing with the pace of his treatments. My husband had never run a marathon but he has watched and cheered me on many times. The mental part he faced was real. I could sense the fatigue. He told me he didn't sleep well last night. He woke up several times in the night sweating and having weird dreams. I listened. I tried to keep his chin up. We were so close but I felt we were hitting the wall…

Parenting is hard. It was even harder during this season. I prayed for patience and compassion most days. Dear *Lord, please give me patience and compassion. Guard my mouth, so that nothing comes out that isn't uplifting. Please give me courage and strength as I care for my family. Amen.*

I recall one evening asking my son to brush his teeth. He pounded the wall. I was shocked. He yelled, "Stop nagging me, Mom!"

I froze. He turned his back to me, marched into his room, and shut the door.

I understood it had nothing to do with his teeth and everything with his Dad being sick.

Deep breath.

I knocked on his door and was thankful he let me come in.

He shouted, "Strike three for you, Mom!"

He was sitting on his bed as I walked over to him and sat down. I didn't know what to say, so I kept my mouth shut. I hugged him instead.

I was grateful he let me and didn't pull away. I squeezed him tight for a moment. When I let go he went to the bathroom and took care of his teeth. I understood he felt bad about his behavior and there was no need for me to point it out. When he came back into his room, I grabbed a book and we read for a bit.

He seemed in a better place so I went to check on Delaney. It was her bedtime. I read to her and then put her to bed. I went back to Brindsley's room and tucked him in.

Once both kids were to bed I went to check on Jeff. He was lying on the couch in the living room. His eyes were closed as he winced in pain. "I don't want to do another round of chemo, Jules."

I sat on the couch beside him and rubbed his left elbow. He mentioned it was hurting. My heart sank. I didn't want him to endure another round either though both oncologists agreed it was the best way to cure him. My mind groaned, *I hope this works and he doesn't need anymore after round four. I can't imagine going through the summer like this.*

Jeff opened his eyes and looked at me as if he read my mind, "I hope this works. I've had moments when I wonder if this is even working." He winced again and asked for the ice pack over his forehead.

I stopped rubbing his elbow and headed into the kitchen. I looked down the hall to make sure the kids weren't awake. I didn't want them to see Jeff in so much pain. I grabbed an ice pack and sat back down next to Jeff placing it over his forehead.

"My entire body hurts, my thumb feels like it has just been smashed with a hammer and my left elbow hurts, would you keep rubbing it? Why won't this stupid pain pill kick in!"

My mind searched for what else I could do to help him get comfortable. I wanted to offer meditation though I bit my tongue, he has brushed me away when I brought that up before.

I sat with him instead and listened.

"I'm sorry I'm keeping you up" as tears rolled down his cheeks.

"Jeff, I'm okay and want to sit here with you." I continued to massage his left elbow.

He continued, "I didn't want to go to treatment today, I know it was a short day today but I still didn't want to go. I'm getting tired of this and I want my life back. I'm glad to be home with you and the kids but I'm not myself."

I wondered, *will he ever be cured?* I realized that wasn't a helpful question. I changed it to, *will he stay in remission? This could come back and we will be going through this all over again. I don't know if I can go through this again. The drugs they were putting in his body gave him a high likelihood he could get some other type of cancer.*

My mind raced from one thought to another. I was starting to go down into the black. I had to redirect my thoughts. *Fight back Julie, he is going to be okay and if it comes back you will be ready.*

I grabbed Jeff's hand and was still. I listened. I wanted him to let out what was on his mind. I kept quiet and hushed my mind.

He continued…and I sat and listened.

I woke up the next day not feeling well. A cold was coming on and I was hopeful I wouldn't pass this on to Jeff. He had one more round. I was worried if he got sick it would delay his last 21-day cycle of treatment. He didn't seem concerned. He felt so poor and shrugged off my distress.

I kept my distance anyway. I promised myself I would take a nap and double down on the fruits and veggies. Aunt Phoebe squeaked in— "Well you haven't cleaned the bathroom in a week and you've been eating too much sugar." There goes the judge. I laughed to myself. *Sometimes we get sick— I did nothing wrong.* I wasn't going to let those negative thoughts distract me.

Yes, the bathrooms needed to be cleaned and I would get to that after I took a nap. I was enjoying the chocolate-covered strawberries gifted to us. Yet not in an over-indulging way— chocolate was bringing me joy! It was a yummy treat the kids and I gathered around the table to snack on while we talked about our day. I was grateful for Carrie-Anne and Debi who sent these delicious treats.

Jeff was sitting at the kitchen table. I sat at the other end with my breakfast. I didn't want to get him sick. I ate while he voiced his concerns about the chemotherapy drugs on his lungs. He was reading that one drug could cause pulmonary fibrosis. I could tell this was weighing on his mind. He may not get it now but it could show up later in life and there wasn't much treatment for it but a lung transplant. I forgot about this information in the chemotherapy teaching session, maybe I only remembered what I wanted to hear.

Worry wasn't useful but I did it for both of us. My mind raced to— what does that mean for our future, for travel, for the kids? Does this mean his life will be cut short or he won't be as healthy as he could have been? Does it mean cancer again or more appointments in the future?

My inner coach stepped in—okay, now tell the flip side to all the worries above. Jeff recovers from cancer, it doesn't come back, he regains his health and strength, he lives a healthy, happy life full of travel, and lives a long time to see our children grow up.

I would rather tell myself this story— *Jeff will return to good health and will live a long life ahead.*

I recall what a church member had said to me when we learned Jeff was sick, "Set down all your worries and cares at the foot of Jesus and do not turn around to pick them back up."

The last part of what she said was powerful, "Do not turn around to pick them back up." I do that. I set down my worries but then I turn around. I think I will handle it better or faster and grab them again to carry the load myself.

Why do I do this? I'm human I suppose but I want to trust. I want to trust God is with me and I don't have to carry these worries. I can give them to Him.

* * *

We saw Dr. Duffy after the third cycle. Jeff shared the struggles with the Neulasta— awful bone pain and heaviness. Dr. Duffy decided to hold off on the Neulasta for the last cycle. Jeff was very pleased and relieved. We were going to stick to the regimen of drugs even though the hearing had declined. His pulmonary function was good so he didn't think we should switch drugs. He said, "Let's stick to one more round. If we end now it just may not be enough to cure you and that is what we want." I was beginning to believe this was possible.

I prayed this was the case for Jeff. It was hard to accept fully since we understood the side effects of the chemotherapy drugs— the potential risk for cancer later in life being the biggest worry. Yet I couldn't let my mind worry about the future. *Julie, be present in this moment for this is what is here. Rejoice and be glad.*

It's Your Move:
Push-Ups and Laughter
Check out the It's Your Move channel: www.youtube.com/@juliebhughes

CHAPTER 31

ANGELS RUN

First 5K Run
The start has begun.
Stride for stride
her arms and
legs come alive
Weaving through the crowd
She smiles—
Mom I got up the hill
how much longer now?
Silly conversations
to sidetrack tired
legs and pain.
Reassuring her—
walking is okay.
Counting cones to keep
her moving—
One, two, three...

The cheers roaring
A downhill soaring
The finish is in sight—
Kick it in with all
your might.
A gift today for this mother runner—
A daughter to run alongside
My heart is full of pride.

Brindsley, Delaney, and I registered for The 5K Good Samaritan Run. We organized a team called Healthy, Happy, and Strong. We recruited friends and family to join us. I was grateful Jeff felt good enough to come and cheer us on. He had just finished his third round of chemotherapy treatment. I had no idea what each day would bring, or how he would feel, so for him to come was a blessing.

He bundled up in a hat, jacket, gloves, and a smile. He was a trooper. We parked the car close to the event in case he needed to sit in the car. My mom met us there. She decided to hang with Jeff as the kids and I ran.

I was grateful to see some friends I hadn't seen in a while. One family in particular was there and I hadn't shared with them what we were going through. I made a mental note to call them later.

Delaney and I planned to run the 5K together. My friends Felicia and Jeanne also joined us. This was Delaney's first 5K, so it was enjoyable for all of us to run as a group. Brindsley lined up at the start with some of his friends and two of his teachers. I was happy to see Brindsley surrounded by his buddies and teachers, knowing he felt supported. I was filled with joy seeing that he had this network of support participating with him.

The race director yelled, Go! Brindsley took off. We ran at Delaney's pace encouraging her every step. When she wanted to pick up the pace, we did too. When she wanted to walk, we did so with enthusiasm.

It made me think of Jeff as he was going through chemotherapy treatment. He was surrounded by his family, healthcare team, church family, co-workers, and friends— we were his pacers. *Keep placing one foot in front of the other— step by step we will be right here.*

* * *

Angels run
I believe they do
I've witnessed
some in races
It's true!

Always there for others

Angels Run

Cheering from behind
Or carrying a runner
to the finish line.

My son ran a 5K
He experienced it too!
He said he heard an
Angel behind him—
Coaching him along
just when he didn't know
what to do—
just squeeze between them, find a gap

She was there
to encourage him too
It's okay— Go, you're doing great!
Brindsley picked up his pace
He didn't wait.
She eased his mind
His confidence shined

And this mother runner
was happy to behold
that her son got to run
with an angel
And was never alone

I loved the conversation Brindsley shared with me after the race.

"Hey Mom, there was an angel behind me helping me in the race." Brindsley's smile was as wide as the sky.

"Oh really! That's awesome buddy, tell me all about it."

"I was running behind some adults and I didn't know how to get around them. I heard someone from behind me say, just squeeze between them and find a gap. It was like she read my mind, it was my angel Mom!"

"Oh cool, Brindsley! Angels are running with us, I'm so glad she helped you."

My heart was full, another win for the week. Not only did my children have fun and finish the race, but they witnessed angels—they were gaining evidence that they were never alone. *There is kindness and good all around. Which we all needed right now.*

* * *

When we arrived home a van pulled into our driveway a few minutes later. It was my friend and her family that I planned on calling. They dropped off a gift basket that Delaney won in the raffle at the race. *God's timing is always right.* I could now tell her in person. Her children came in to use the bathroom and Jenny asked with concerned eyes, "Is Jeff sick?"

How did she know? Jeff still was very thin and had no facial hair though he did have a hat on. We stood outside and I shared with her what was going on. She hugged me and said she would lift our family in prayer. Jeff was sharing the news with her husband at the same time.

Before they left, we held hands in our driveway, closed our eyes, and bowed our heads. Her children patiently waited in the car. I held back tears as Dan lifted us in prayer. Their kindness, faith, trust, and love will never be forgotten. I was thankful Delaney entered the raffle and she won.

* * *

Sunday's run was at the Erie Canal Trail. I loved this spot to run, not only did it give me a break from the hills but there was always somebody to see. Blue herons, cardinals, deer, and sometimes we would spot a beaver, snapping turtle, or wild turkey.

Felicia and I were on our way back when we spotted a woman on the trail looking at something. She was standing close to the edge of the bank looking down at the water. As I got closer I was curious about what she was so interested in. We stopped once we caught up to her. I asked, "What are you looking at?"

"I think it's a beaver, what do you think?"

Felicia and I stepped closer and looked down at the water. An enormous brown ball

136

waddled towards the edge. I recognized the tail.

"Yup, that's a beaver! How cool."

The beaver entered the water and all three of us stood there in silence as we watched the beaver swim across to the other side. I had no idea how fascinating it was to watch a beaver swim. The tail moving up and down in the water was mesmerizing. Slow and steady the beaver climbed out of the water and made his way up the bank. He was so big and cute from a distance. I grinned.

The woman turned to us, "The early bird catches the worm, glad I'm on the trail early to see him this morning."

We nodded and smiled. I chimed in, "That's why we love running so early, there's so much we get to see."

We waved goodbye and began our run again.

I was content. I loved being among creation, it made me feel like everything was right in the world.

Everything will be okay.

It's Your Move:
Bird-Dog Exercise
Check out the It's Your Move channel: www.youtube.com/@juliebhughes

CHAPTER 32

ONE MORE ROUND

A doctor's visit with
my husband
We've been here before
Will they ever end
Or is there more in store
The clinic is packed
So many people
Enduring the fight
I want to hug or squeeze
each person's hand
with all my might.
A cure is what
We are after
to feel like himself again
Hard for me to imagine
with the poison dripping in
Every cell in his body
taking it on
And we pray
it's doing the job
The Doc says this will do it
Just one more round.
This will be a tough month
Yet you've made it this far.
Tears come
Cancer changes everything

Nothing will be the same
Yet what really ever stays the same?
We'll grow through
this season of fire
and pain.
The rising will come

Dr. Duffy wanted to check in with Jeff's symptoms, look over his blood work, and confirm the plan moving forward. This was something we were now accustomed to. We would meet with him after every cycle and this one wasn't much different except there was light at the end of the tunnel. One more round.

Dr. Duffy brought his enthusiasm and tried to pump Jeff up. He was calm, kind, and had the spirit we desperately needed that day. He offered encouragement and support as Jeff opened up about his mental fatigue and not wanting to continue with the treatment. His third round was a struggle. He was exhausted. Nothing like the first two cycles. The side effects of the drugs were starting to wear on him and mentally he was drained. He didn't want to do anymore but he knew he must... *One more round.*

I prayed for his strength and resilience. I prayed for my patience and energy as we endured this last round. *I think we have a long road ahead after chemotherapy is over. He will need time to heal and recover. He will need time to process what his body and mind have been through. Some of the side effects may stay and that will be something we will need to face and reconcile. We will need time to grieve.*

I wrote this poem after my run. I needed strength after today's visit and the wind was happy to help me. Thank you wind. Thank you, Great Creator.

Four miles
Easy, peasy
I say.
The wind builds and
Shouts
I want to play!
I roll my eyes
It's NOT what
I had in mind.

One More Round

The wind is strong—
nudging me side to side
Yet the cool breeze
feels great
over the long
months of freeze
Okay, Wind—
I will play
But in return
would you please
give me some of your
strength today?
I feel a giant push
from behind
as I begin my climb.
Thank you, Wind.

* * *

I imagined my family and I were at mile 24 of Jeff's chemotherapy treatments. We were almost to the finish! We were so close. My children were missing their dad. I was missing my husband.

I hear, "He's always on the couch, he's got chemo (*oops, they think it's chemo and not cancer*) and all he does is sleep."

Sigh…all of this was true.

My gentle reminder, "This is temporary. This will end. There is light at the end of the tunnel."

Then an idea came to me. What timing.

"Hey, let's plan a party."

Oh, they loved hearing this. My daughter Delaney got out her notebook and started making a list of what we needed. Balloons, snacks, music…

It turned the entire mood around as we gathered around the kitchen table to plan the celebration—*Jeff enduring four rounds of chemotherapy.* I found a cardboard sign in the closet and Brindsley got out the markers.

"Let's make a sign for Dad." They smiled in agreement as we all got to work.

Brindsley worked on one side and Delaney on the other. I stood back for a moment thankful this was all it took to change the direction of the day.

We laughed as we looked at the finished product. Brindsley added his stuffed animal remarks to the poster board. "Jeff-Jeff (*his stuffed animal dog*) had been cheering you on the moment you started chemo!" and "Simba knew you could do it!" Delaney drew hearts and stars on her side with the words "The legend, the myth, Dad!" and "You are the best Dad ever!"

I was filled with joy reading what they came up with. The last time they made a sign was for me crossing The Boston Marathon finish line. Today, they made a sign for Dad crossing his personal marathon, finishing four rounds of chemotherapy.

Delaney hid the sign in her closet and I told her I would be in charge of balloons. She smiled.

***

When I looked at the calendar for the week ahead I saw Jeff added something. On May 9th, 2022 he wrote "Last day of chemo B—es!!" Jeff's last chemotherapy treatment. Hallelujah! I was not going to miss the drive to and from his treatments. I was happy this was it for a while— a break.

I decided to get the balloons that morning after I dropped him off. He had no idea what we had planned. Balloons, a homemade sign, and some treats. We were going to celebrate.

I stepped into the Dollar Store surprised by how busy it was. I waited in line to order the balloons. I wanted to get a big bunch of them. When it was my turn I told her how many balloons I wanted. She paused and mentioned, "You should have ordered ahead of time."

I was embarrassed. I didn't think to call ahead. I told her I would come back. I looked behind me to see a line, four deep.

She replied, "No, no, it is fine." Though I felt it wasn't.

As I waited in line for my over-the-top order of balloons the woman behind me asked, "Are you having a party."

I turned to her and smiled, "Yes, we are celebrating my husband's last day of chemotherapy treatment. My kids and I thought lots of balloons would help."

When the words came out, *the last day of chemotherapy*, tears did too. I didn't hold them back like so many times during this challenge. I let them come as I stood there in line. The four women behind me didn't say a word.

I felt a sense of space being offered to me. I didn't know how to explain it other than I knew God was with me. I felt safe. The lady who asked was kind and wished me well. I stood in the line tears on my cheeks as I watched the cashier blow up each balloon.

I took a deep breath, smiled, and thanked everyone for their patience. I was the reason for the hold-up as I gathered the balloons. I walked out feeling a little bit lighter. The red, blue, and orange balloons shined in the sun as I gently placed them in the car. We made it four rounds!

Deep breath.

I put my seatbelt on and started the car. We made it through this storm and I believed we would come out the other side wiser, stronger, and kinder.

It's Your Move:
Slider with Shoulder Shrugs
Check out the It's Your Move channel: www.youtube.com/@juliebhughes

CHAPTER 33

HUGHES STRONG

Our light in the darkness
Miracle worker
God, you are both
Our strength when we are weak.
Troubles will come
We don't need to worry
You are here
You will never leave
You are everywhere
Thank you, Jesus.

Jeff had a few rough days after his last round. He continued to complain of fatigue and weakness. I heard him should-ing on himself, "I shouldn't be this tired still, I haven't done anything today." "I should be doing something." "Why am I still so nauseous?"

What he felt and experienced, the doctor said was to be expected for a few more months. Dr. Duffy was very honest and told us what to expect as each round continued. What Jeff would experience and what would happen. He was spot-on each time. I remembered that as he told us about the next few months. Even though chemotherapy was finished the side effects would linger. He reminded us, "It's going to take a while to get back to feeling better."

I heard what Dr. Duffy said though it didn't sink in. I believed he would bounce right back after the chemotherapy stopped— everything would go back to normal. *I couldn't have been more wrong.*

I expected after treatment stopped, Jeff would be Jeff. I wanted to see a difference. I felt ashamed expecting him to recover overnight. I knew better. I needed to be patient with his body and mind. I just wanted my husband back. He was still sleeping on the couch and having a hard time getting up. He was weak. I was frustrated.

* * *

Dr. Duffy wanted Jeff to hold off from starting any formal exercise program until the CT scan and endoscopy were completed and the results were in. The doctor scheduled the procedures four weeks after Jeff's last chemotherapy treatment. I wanted to hear zero cancer cells...remission. The word cure I was not interested in. I'd heard cure before and look what we just went through. *Nothing is certain.*

Jeff agreed to keep his port in just in case treatment needed to start up again. Dr. Duffy mentioned he would like him to leave it in for a year if it wasn't too much trouble or hassle. Jeff agreed.

We prayed for zero cancer cells. Who wants to go through this again? Not us. I was trying not to worry and to keep an optimistic attitude. Meanwhile, Jeff was planning on when he could get back to work. I was surprised by this. It seemed too soon to think about work. Was he bored? Worried about money? I didn't know but the doctor encouraged him to think about going back part-time, and gradually work back into his normal routine. I knew my husband wasn't going to follow those recommendations. It wasn't my place to tell him what to do though I did voice my agreement with the doctor.

"Jeff please give yourself time to recover. Don't rush back into work."

He nodded, "I will but I need to get my life back."

I trusted he would go back when he felt good enough. The doctor mentioned it would take a few years to fully feel himself. It was hard to hear.

I was praying hard. Praying the cancer was gone so we could get Jeff back. Praying he would not need to endure any more chemotherapy. Praying he could start to recover, exercise, and build his stamina and strength.

* * *

146

Cathy dropped Jeff off for his upper endoscopy. I would pick him up when the nurse called me. I was glad she was available to help us. I was grateful to get a break from dropping him off. I believe my mother-in-law was happy to help. As a mother, I could only imagine what she must be feeling and thinking. If this were my son, *how would I respond?* I was thankful for her strength.

She arrived at 6:45 a.m. with her coffee mug in hand and a smile. The kids were still sleeping. I was grateful I didn't have to wake them up. Jeff gathered his things before heading out the door with his Mom. I was thankful she was someone we could rely on.

Once Brindsley and Delaney were ready for school I dropped them off and headed to the Erie Canal trail for a run. The trail was a combination of gravel and pavement, parallel to the water. A great place to calm my nerves as Jeff was having his procedure.

I started before the rain hoping I would beat it when a bicyclist approached me making conversation, "Do you think we will beat the rain?"

"Doesn't look like it. Maybe we will get a few drops," I replied.

I looked to my right and spotted a huge snapping turtle sitting along the side of the bank. The biker was just ahead, he saw it too. I let out "Wow, look at that snapping turtle!"

He looked back at me on his bike and slowed down a bit, "Oh yes, they come up to the bank every year and lay their eggs, I've seen the babies before."

"That is awesome, maybe I will get a chance to see them too. Have a great bike ride," I called.

"How far are you running today?" he called back.

"Seven miles." I raised my voice a bit so he could hear me as he pedaled.

"Great! Have fun," and off he went.

I was still in awe from spotting the snapping turtle. I was so glad I got the chance to see it this morning. The raindrops started to hit my arms as I crossed over the bridge to get on the main trail. The rain felt nice. The smell was my favorite. I always loved running in the rain. The thought must have been heard by the clouds as it began to pour for the next 15 minutes of my run. I laughed to myself— *be careful what you wish for.*

I was splashing in the puddles on the gravel path and weaving around the geese's droppings. I looked up to see a family of them to my right. The baby goslings with their parents all huddled together pecking at the ground. They were adorable. My heart sang. I loved the birds and wildlife I encountered—*it's magnificent.*

I ran past them as the parents eyed me ready to hiss. They were so protective of their young. I'd learned on my many runs to keep my distance. I looked down at my watch just as the rain let up —time to turn around.

I headed back, and a dozen bicyclists passed me as we said good morning and hello. I was glad to see so many people out moving on this rainy morning acknowledging each other. I crossed over the bridge and kept my eye out for the snapping turtle again— maybe it was still on the bank—they do move slowly, right? I kept my eyes on the lookout but didn't see that turtle again—maybe next time.

I checked my phone to see if the nurse called. Not yet. My mind raced to the worst-case scenarios— *oh great, why is this taking so long? I wonder if something is wrong.* I rolled my eyes. *Everything is fine, maybe they didn't start the procedure on time.*

Deep breath.

I decided to drive to the clinic and wait in my car until I got the call. I could write and read while I waited. I sat in the parking lot for what seemed like hours when my phone finally rang.

"Hello."

"Hi, Julie, Jeff is all set and everything went great. You can meet us outside the front entrance. I will wheel him out."

"Okay, great, I'm here and will pull up to the front. Thank you so much."

I was relieved to hear they didn't need me to come in. I took that as a sign that everything looked good. I pulled up to the entrance as Jeff was being wheeled out to the sidewalk. He stood and got into the car with ease.

He smiled. "I'm sorry that took so long. My fingers were so cold and white. They couldn't get my oxygen reading. I had to run my hands under warm water before they could start the procedure."

"I wondered why it was taking so long. I was getting nervous."

"The doctor said everything looked good when she was in there. She took a lot of tissue to sample to make sure no cancer cells were left."

"Okay, good. Do you want to stop and get some food?"

"No, I'm really tired and just want to go home and sleep."

* * *

We would see the gastrointestinal doctor the following week to learn of the results of the scope. I was hoping if the doctor did see something out of the ordinary she would let us know. She planned to take some of the cells in and around the duodenum and have them biopsied. I was happy to hear she was sending the biopsies to the same person who examined them in January.

The CT scan was the next day. We had an appointment with Dr. Duffy at the end of the week to go over the results. I was relieved we would at least know something by the end of the week. Jeff mentioned work and he wondered if he would be able to return by the end of the summer. I was happy he was giving himself time to recover. I didn't want to get ahead of ourselves until we got the results. I was curious about what the doctor would say about his plan.

Jeff tried his best to play with the kids more since chemotherapy ended. He admitted it was a struggle. He didn't feel strong or steady. His appetite wasn't great. His taste was still off and his stomach was too. He mentioned a lot of cramping and tightness in his abdomen. He had lost some of his hearing and would have moments when his tinnitus was extremely distressing.

I recalled asking him to turn off the oven one evening when the timer went off. I was leaving the house to take Brindsley to an activity. Jeff said, "Okay." I figured he understood and heard me.

When I arrived home the timer was off but the oven was still on and the baking sheet of food was still inside. The food cooked more than I wanted. When I asked him why he didn't turn the oven off he shrugged, all he heard was turn the timer off. This made me concerned but I tried not to show it. I could tell Jeff was bothered by it and upset with himself.

I noticed during this time, moments when he truly didn't hear me and moments when he did but it took him a while to process what he heard. We scheduled an appointment for hearing aids. I began researching the effects chemotherapy had on the brain. I didn't have much luck with the latter. The one thing I did find over and over was the phrase "Brain fog or Chemo brain." What Jeff was experiencing was not out of the ordinary.

They don't talk about it enough— the effects chemotherapy has on the brain. Jeff's processing, speed, and comprehension were all influenced by the drugs. I realized at this moment his road to recovery may be a long one. I would need to be patient.

Deep breath.

The great thing about being an endurance runner was the ability to sustain hardship for a prolonged period—*there are no shortcuts*—keep putting one foot in front of the other. *I'm relating this cancer journey very similarly.* It helped me. This had been my way of coping with his diagnosis and treatment. It was a way for me to keep moving forward, not to get stuck in despair. *This is temporary. We will make it through this storm and come out the other side wiser, stronger, and kinder.* I wanted to believe this last affirmation deep in my bones. I repeat it here in case you do too.

Patience, persistence, and courage we continued to pray for as we awaited the results. I was praying today was when Jeff would have the opportunity to start his comeback.

Hughes Strong!

It's Your Move:
Single Leg Raise: Front and Side
Check out the It's Your Move channel: www.youtube.com/@juliebhughes

CHAPTER 34

RUN FOR JEFF

Three loops
Ten-plus miles each
Mud, roots, dirt
Under my feet
I can do this
Nature has my back
Sights, sound, smell
Mindset on track
I have what it takes
Breathe, relax, run
31 miles to victory
Remember to have fun!

I smiled in disbelief at my watch—31.83 miles! *I did it.*

I had three goals for my first 50K trail run— Run the third loop if I make the cut-off time, focus on my nutrition each loop, and finish with a smile. Oh!, and don't faceplant in the mud.

My mom had the kids all morning so I didn't feel rushed to get home. I planned to run the entire three loops which meant I would be gone for most of the day. Jeff would have a quiet home to rest and recover. The kids would enjoy their time with Nana. I needed this time alone in the woods. My friend and run buddy, Felicia was going to run too.

The first loop was relaxed with lots of conversation and laughter. We met a runner from Manhattan, New York. She was full of energy and enjoyed the company. "I'm usually running all by myself, this is great to run with you all." She wore a smile. "I'm happy to be out of the city."

We met a local runner whose goal was to run three loops. She was happy to hear we were too. Her dad caught up with us. It was nice to hear the conversation from behind. We were all together. Many of the runners there were doing one loop but a few runners mentioned they were aiming for three. I was happy to know more runners were continuing.

When the first climb approached us everyone stopped and power walked. I was surprised by this— not at all like a road race. If I wanted to make it three loops I needed to embrace the idea of walking the steep hills. I left my ego in the car. I walked too. I was new at this. These runners were experienced. They had several trail races and ultras under their belt. I was going to watch and follow their lead.

The first loop we made in a great time. I was happy with how I felt and had no doubt about continuing. We entered the trail for our second loop as the rain started to fall. My mind focused on the gentle noise covering us as we ducked under branches and stepped over logs.

The sound was soothing, keeping us on pace. The more I ran the more I listened to nature and not to my thoughts. It was a great distraction for me as we started another ten-mile loop. My focus turned to the pine needle smell, the beautiful bright green ferns along the trail, and the tall trees surrounding us. My heart was filled with appreciation. Memories of hiking with my uncle and childhood camp entered my mind. *I love the trails. I love the woods.* I felt like a kid again sloshing through the mud, crossing and hopping over the streams. I felt free.

As we made our way to the start/finish line once again, the clock read just over four hours. YES! We made the cut-off time. *We've got one more loop!*

As I crossed the start/finish line several runners were gathered cheering me in. It was great to see everyone though I wasn't done. I stopped at the picnic table to grab more hydration bottles before heading back onto the trail for the last loop. The race director checked in with me. I gave him the thumbs up that I was continuing. I made the cut-off time!

I was committed to the last loop and thrilled I had the opportunity to go for it. I guzzled down half of the new bottles as I entered the trail one last time alone.

I was hopeful the women runners behind me would catch up. I made sure to pay extra attention to the turns and trail markings now that I was on my own. I coached myself through the last loop. I was prepared for the negative thoughts to show up. I was ready. *I can do this, just one more loop. Relax, breathe, and run. I am strong.* I turned my focus on the sounds, sights, and smells to distract me from the discomfort.

As I ran up to a large mud pit at about mile 27, I saw two hikers heading in my direction. It was nice to see people on the trail. They stood there trying to decide if they wanted to venture into the mud or not. I kept running toward them and the lady yelled out, "Be careful it's so muddy and you don't want to slip."

I realized she was just being kind but I had to laugh as my legs were covered in mud and this was my third time through. I smiled and replied, "Thank you." It felt good to laugh and it was comforting to see other people. I was almost done!

I had about four more miles to go and continued my mantras to get me to the finish. As I ran towards the last bridge I took a quick look at my watch, I was just over 6 hours. I could make it in under 6 hours and 10 minutes. Go! Go! Go!

I ran up the stone steps and made a right turn up the gravel lot towards the finish. I ran with all I had left and crossed the finish in 6 hours and 9 minutes! My first 50K was achieved. Thank you body and mind! *We did it.*

I was tired. I was glad I could stand and take in hydration while we waited for the rest of the runners to finish. A feeling of sadness came over me— I wished my family was here. Yet I looked forward to telling them all about the morning and my experience at my first ultra trail race.

* * *

In my memoir, *Staring Down a Dream: A Mom, a Marathoner, a Mission,* one of the main themes of the book was the power of our mindset not only in running but in life. I was reminded of this once again when I lined up for the 50K trail race.

Two weeks before the race, I got sick and couldn't run for ten days. Since I missed so much training time, I wasn't sure if I could complete the entire race distance. I reflected on the consistent training I had done before getting sick and decided I could still finish if I stayed determined. I told myself that as long as I met the halfway cutoff time, I would keep running no matter what. I believed that staying positive and focusing on my mental strength could push me through the final 10 miles. It worked! Repeating positive mantras to myself helped me complete the last loop faster than I had originally planned.

Can I do another loop?—yes I can and I will. I'm strong, I have what it takes and I will run this last loop for Jeff. He just finished four rounds of chemo—*I'm running this last loop for him. I can handle this discomfort. I will keep going.*

When my mind worried— *you should have stopped or are you sure you can do this alone?* I stayed calm, repeated my mantras, and enjoyed my surroundings. I let go of any expectations other than to finish. I was happy I had the opportunity to run the third loop. Despite the setback from being sick, my positive mindset and trust in my prior training helped me achieve my goal.

I could have believed the story that because I'd been sick for ten days and didn't run I had no business running a 50K. Instead, I believed this story—*I've got enough training under my belt. I've run marathons. I feel really strong today and I've been on the trails enough. I can do this.*

I talked myself into running the third loop and proved to myself, once again, that what I say to myself, what I believe matters. It was my secret power. *I can handle being uncomfortable and not freak out. I can manage my mind and focus on moving forward.*

It's Your Move:
Goblet March
Check out the It's Your Move channel: www.youtube.com/@juliebhughes

CHAPTER 35

MIRACLE WORKER

A champion—
You never gave up
When it knocked you down
You got back up

Stood firm
In His power
Ready for another round
Cancer—doesn't stand a chance
God's grace and love
will turn this around.

Holding you up
His strength
will carry you through
Great is
His faithfulness—
He is always with you.

You are brave
A mighty Warrior—
A Hero—
We love you!

I was exhausted— mentally more than physically. My mind replayed these questions— *is it gone? Is it still in his body? Will he need more treatment?* My prayer was that it would never come back. Jeff had his endoscopy and CT scan, and now we wait. I thought I was patient but these last few days are proving otherwise. I was hopeful the four rounds of chemotherapy did the job and the good news was on the horizon.

I wanted our lives back to when Jeff was present, full of energy, and playful with the kids. I wanted to get back to being us. This challenge had taken so much from us these last several months yet staying in that mental space was not helpful. It made me feel sick. I needed to reframe that view— *what it's given us, what I've learned, and the blessings that have come from this difficult time.* I reflected on these questions instead.

I'm going to sit with these today. Instead of becoming anxious and worried, I will begin to write down and consider the gifts, the joy, and the silver lining of these last several months.

I wasn't ready to answer all these questions yet, but I wrote them down. My curiosity grew. I started with— what did I learn? I learned that receiving was important and okay. I learned how to accept with a cheerful heart and not pull away. The generosity of family, friends, members of the writing community, and perfect strangers who showed up for us taught me this.

* * *

I had trouble falling asleep as I worried about Jeff's results. I kept pleading as I tossed and turned, *please let the scans be clear, please Lord have the cancer be zero.* I eventually fell asleep, but woke up to find Jeff not in bed beside me. He had moved to the couch in the middle of the night, which was a common occurrence that I had come to accept. I wished he would stay in bed with me. He said he couldn't get comfortable and would wake up unable to fall back asleep, so his solution was to go to the couch.

When I came out to the living room he was already awake and on the iPad. I figured he was looking at sports scores but he asked me to come over, "I have something to show you."

I looked at the screen. It was his CT scan results. They were already posted to his chart on the patient portal. We would be heading to Dr. Duffy this morning to find out his results however here they were on the screen. I couldn't believe it. I stared in disbelief at the words.

I looked at Jeff, "Oh my gosh, the scan looks good!"

"Yes, this is great news!"

I hugged him. The CT Scans were negative. Thank you, Lord. Thank you for answering our prayers.

* * *

Jeff drove us to his appointment that morning. It felt great to be the passenger. I wondered how Jeff felt driving to his oncologist instead of riding shotgun. We arrived at his appointment lighter knowing the results were in our favor.

We sat next to each other waiting for Dr. Duffy to come in. I began to cry, tears landing on my disposable mask. Jeff held my hand. *Why am I crying?* I was happy. I was relieved. I was thankful. I could see the light at the end of the tunnel getting brighter.

I took some deep breaths, trying to get my body to relax and for the tears to stop. I wanted to gain my composure before Dr. Duffy arrived. I wanted to be focused and attentive to what he would share. What would be Jeff's next steps?

Dr. Duffy's first words as he entered the room were, "Jeff your scans look good and so does your blood work. I want to wait on the biopsy results but Jeff I think the treatment got it."

I smiled under my mask. Even though we already knew the results, it was reassuring to hear it out loud from the doctor.

He went over the results and asked Jeff to follow up with him in three months for another CT Scan and more blood work. It sounded like this would be Jeff's course of action for a while, scans and blood work every three months. Dr. Duffy emphasized the importance of rest and recovery. He would like him to wait a while longer on returning to work and wait a few more weeks before starting any formal exercise program.

He ended the visit with, "Jeff you are in remission." The words comforted me. I continued my prayers over the weekend as we awaited the biopsy results. We would meet with the gastrointestinal doctor the following week. I was praying for more good news.

* * *

I had a sudden unease in my stomach as we sat in the gastrointestinal doctor's office. Jeff and I were silent as we waited for her to come in. My mind racing…*if this is positive maybe Jeff will just need to do one or two more rounds, and we can do it BUT if it's negative—please be negative I don't want him to have any more drugs.*

My thoughts were interrupted by the door opening. The doctor walked in carrying her laptop. I was certain she was smiling under her mask. She sat down across from us and announced, "The biopsy is clear, it looks good Jeff!"

I let out an exhale—tears landing on my disposable mask. I smiled. I turned to Jeff who was sitting on the treatment table. I grabbed his hand and squeezed it. I was able to keep my composure so I could hear and focus on what she had to say. Jeff's posture relaxed. She showed us the pictures and shared the results.

The biopsy was negative. The cancer cells were gone—only scar tissue remained. She took her time going over everything with us and what to expect moving forward. She wanted to perform another upper endoscopy in six months. I couldn't stop smiling.

Jeff voiced his questions and gratitude for her care before we got up to leave. She gave us both a hug. We were so happy. I felt lighter. I felt like I could breathe deeper. It was now time to focus on his recovery and doing things as a family again. We could officially celebrate! Jeff's scans and biopsy were negative—**ZERO cancer cells remain!**

Jeff was relieved. He admitted, "I was nervous, I'm so glad I don't have to do any more chemo."

We hugged and then called our moms to tell them the great news. Praise the Lord! God was still in the business of miracles. *Thank you, Lord.*

It's Your Move:
Hamstring Isometric and Hamstring Isometric With March
Check out the It's Your Move channel: www.youtube.com/@juliebhughes

CHAPTER 36

TORTOISE OR THE HARE?

I woke up at 5 a.m. to head out for my run and saw a brown paper bag on the counter. *What is this?* I looked in the empty bag and found a receipt. The time on it was 9:38 p.m. *Oh, Jeff what did you need so late?* I scanned the receipt and to my horror read peanut butter brownies printed twice. *He bought two pans of brownies?* Sigh…so much for fruit and vegetables.

I didn't say anything when he woke up. I didn't tell him I knew until later that evening. We got a good laugh. It seemed like a long time since we had sat together and laughed. It felt good. He thought I didn't know about it. *I'm on to him!* He thought he was sneaky and secretive but I knew the entire time.

He just went through four rounds of chemotherapy, he'd been through hell…he could enjoy a pan of peanut butter brownies, right? *Nothing is worse than the poison he endured for four months.*

"How did you know?" He grinned as I told him about the bag, receipt, oh and the knife in the sink with chocolate all over it.

"I was eating them for breakfast when you came in with the groceries, I was hoping you didn't notice."

I laughed or at least I tried. I didn't know he was eating them for breakfast but I already knew they were in the house. I wanted Jeff to eat healthier. He was aware of the changes he would need to make. I practiced patience once again. I vowed to not get upset or frustrated about his choices.

I turned to writing. My hand raced along the page with frustration and annoyance. It had been a tough few days for me and now peanut butter brownies for breakfast. I'd been irritable— reacting instead of responding. I didn't like it one bit.

At the beginning of the week, my mom came over and I freaked out on her for the stupidest thing. I apologized, but still, I felt terrible. I was disappointed in myself. I didn't show up how I wanted to.

What was that all about? Why did I just freak out? I sat on my bed taking some deep breaths to calm down. *Maybe I'm tired? Maybe these last few months are now catching up to me.* Or the fact that Jeff was still on the couch. *Jeff please get up and get going. Jeff, please hang out with us.* These thoughts swirled in my mind.

Then with no warning, my thoughts switched to— *you're a terrible mom.* This year challenged my self-confidence and motherhood. A spiral of self-doubt consumed me. *I'm not doing enough. I'm not teaching them enough. I'm failing them.*

What the heck! My mind could be so outrageous. I was scared. *Where is this coming from?*

I felt I was still parenting alone. I had this idea that Jeff would step in after chemotherapy. He would be ready to team up with me and help with the kids. I was wrong and foolish to think in a blink of an eye Jeff would be back to himself. I felt like he was in a post-chemo fog if there was such a thing. *Which now I know there is and it's real.*

He was stuck to the couch. I wanted to scream at him to get up and get going. He was complaining about how stiff he was and how his hands tingled. I wanted to help him yet I was lost on how much to push and intervene.

I asked, "What do you want to do about your stiffness?"

He answered, "Maybe I need to do yoga or stretches."

As a physical therapist, I did have some knowledge on where he could start, and what he could do. I had offered this to him—now it was up to him to take action. I wanted him to take action. Yet I waited and it was frustrating. It wasn't up to me.

Are you the tortoise or the hare?

My friend Kym shared this beautiful question with me. It was a blog post she received in her inbox and passed it along. I began reading the first few sentences…was I the hare and Jeff the tortoise?

I paused.

My mind recalled the last few weeks. I wanted Jeff to be doing more for his recovery. I heard about a LIVESTRONG program being offered at the local YMCA—*Why hasn't he joined? I think that would be so good for him. Why is he still on the couch?*

When I had these thoughts guilt and frustration showed up.

Why isn't he eating more fruits and vegetables? He needs to be eating healthier. Oh my gosh! He ate peanut butter brownies for breakfast! I felt panic. I needed to allow him to go at his pace and let go of the idea that my pace was the only way.

Slow and steady wins the race. Pace it don't race it. These were encouraging phrases I would share with my patients. *Why didn't I have this mindset for my husband?* Looking back I think it was fear. I was scared if he didn't change something fast the cancer would return.

Reading the article reassured me. It allowed me to see this circumstance in a new light. I was open to the idea— I was the hare. Jeff was the tortoise. We could both be ourselves. We didn't need to change into anything new. I was grateful Kym taught me this.

We were different. We took life and healing at different speeds. *I must let him recover at his own pace and trust we will meet at the end together. Slow and steady wins the race.*

It's Your Move:
Step Ups: With or Without Dumbbells
Check out the It's Your Move channel: www.youtube.com/@juliebhughes

CHAPTER 37

GOD, TURN IT AROUND

This can't be true— cancer
No, they said it wouldn't come back
Heartsick, tears stream. My children
in the backseat on the way to school
How do I tell them?
God, turn it around.

Four rounds of chemo— is the plan
He lies on the couch day after day,
exhausted—lagging.
My children are sad and upset
Their dad can't play

God, turn it around.
An army of support from around the world,
praying a breakthrough will come
God, do something— I plead.
Don't allow me to raise
our children alone. Please,
God, turn it around.

Hope and joy in a season of challenge
It is possible
He changes everything
He is healing Jeff—one day at a time
A breakthrough has come
God, turned it around.

A song that had a huge impact on me during this season was by Jen Reddick called, God, Turn it Around. I would hear this song as I brought Jeff to the clinic for treatment, on my way to pick him up, or when I went to get Brindsley and Delaney from school. It was a song I could depend on to lift my spirits.

It gave me hope to keep showing up each day for my family. The words would be my affirmation each hour of every day. *He is healing someone. God is doing something. Right now.*

I believed God was reminding me through this song that He was working even when I felt so much uncertainty. He was up to something. Even though I didn't understand why Jeff's cancer returned. I trusted God and his promises. He was working even though I didn't see it yet.

This song brought me peace and comfort. I added it to the playlist of songs that my friend Carrie-Anne had sent me. Jeff would be healed. A breakthrough would come. God would turn it around. I believed.

He wouldn't leave us. *He is healing Jeff right now.* I believed. He moved mountains for us and our family. We wouldn't have gotten through this year without leaning into His truth. *He is for us and with us. He is faithful.*

It was scary to walk through this season. I was grateful we had an army of support to help us keep our eyes fixed on Him. Now, when I hear this song I tear up and smile. He healed Jeff. *He is in remission. All of my hope is in the name of Jesus. Thank you, Jesus, for turning it around.*

If you are going through troubles lean into your Great Creator. He will bring you peace, comfort, and strength as you take one step in front of the other. You are never alone.

* * *

Jeff was in remission. His recovery was slow. His biggest struggle was fatigue, hearing loss, and low energy.

I recall one morning when he was getting ready for work. He found it difficult to get up and get going. His work day started at 8 a.m. and he was still sitting next to me at 7:50. I hugged him. I could see how difficult this was.

I was sitting at the kitchen table, sipping my coffee. Jeff started putting on his sneakers. He sat in silence for a moment before bending down again to lace them up. As he leaned over to tie his shoelaces, he let out a grunt.

I watched him concerned. I noticed the struggle just in this simple motion— a simple activity for most. He sat in silence again after his sneakers were laced. I wished I could do more for him, and give him some of my energy.

Maybe a hug was enough. I wrapped my arms around him and gave him a gentle squeeze. He smiled, "I'll be okay." He turned toward the hallway and yelled goodbye to Brindsley and Delaney. They came running down to hug him and say goodbye.

Brindsley looked at Jeff and said, "May God bless you today, Dad."

I smiled holding back tears. Jeff smiled and hugged him in gratitude.

Yes, May God bless you today. May God be with you.

* * *

Seven months after Jeff's chemotherapy treatment he was complaining of extreme fatigue and low energy. When Dr. Duffy checked his blood work numbers they were not where they should be. He figured his iron levels would be improving by now. The concern and thought was— *is he still bleeding somewhere?*

The gastrointestinal doctor decided to have Jeff come in January 2023 to have a capsule procedure. Jeff would swallow a pill with a camera inside. The camera would roll along through his entire intestines taking pictures as it went. He would then secrete it out. Wild!

We were hoping it would show us more or tell us something. I was praying his body just needed more time to heal. *It's only been seven months?* Yet, the doctors believed the blood work should have improved. I prayed we would enter 2023 with the worst behind us. We lost so much in 2022. I was hopeful the new year would be better.

Yet my mind was focused on this news…*he might still be bleeding somewhere.* I had a hard time shaking this sentence. I was grateful when it was time to pick up the kids from school. My focus must shift and luckily my great Creator also had a trick up His sleeve…snow!

Once we got home we raced outside to heaps and heaps of fresh falling snow. It was a great distraction for me— *why worry when Delaney wants to make a snow train?* The snow was falling fast into huge snowflakes. I lay on my back in the snow and looked up. Brindsley dashed around me with his football. Snowflakes danced on my eyelashes, nose, and cheeks. I laughed and smiled…joy falling right on my face.

Brindsley and Delaney were curious about my fun. They stopped what they were doing to join me. The three of us side by side on our backs in the snow. We laughed together as the storm continued around us. *I can be laughing while in deep dread. I can be hopeful of the new year ahead and scared of what it may bring. I can feel blessed to be a caregiver to Jeff but also exhausted by it. I can keep going… give myself permission to feel all these emotions knowing God's sustaining grace will get me through.*

* * *

A few days later, Jeff got the call we were praying for. The capsule was clear. Nothing was bleeding. Everything looked good. *Thank you, Lord.* He kept the port in for a few more months. In June of 2023, he had it removed. It was another victory. Another step towards recovery. I felt Jeff could finally move forward with his life and begin to regain confidence in his body.

Dr. Duffy mentioned that his recovery would be a rollercoaster ride. He was right. Even though we were now a year and a half from his last chemotherapy, his progress was three steps forward and five steps back. This was the hardest part. There was no linear path, no quick fix, or magic pill. It was going to take time, effort, perseverance, and courage to regain his health. We would be with him every step of the way— together.

Coincidentally, major advancements in testicular cancer treatment occurred in 1974, the year Jeff was born. Before then, only 5% of men survived testicular cancer. Today, thanks to those breakthroughs, the survival rate is over 90%. Jeff is fortunate to be part of the 90%. We feel immense gratitude he had access to modern treatments that saved his life.

We view our story as an opportunity to support others going through similar challenges. By opening up about our experience, we hope to remind people facing cancer that they are not alone on this journey.

Sharing what we went through is our way of extending compassion and community to those who need it. Our story can become a gift if it helps even one person feel less isolated in their struggle.

It's Your Move:

Split Stance Isometrics

Check out the It's Your Move channel: www.youtube.com/@juliebhughes

CHAPTER 38

HOW IS JEFF DOING?

This chapter wasn't originally here but so many of my beta readers were wondering...how is Jeff now?

He is currently two years out from being diagnosed in February of 2022. He is wearing his hearing aids faithfully. He is playing football and basketball with Brindsley and board games, and puzzles with Delaney. He is taking walks and beginning to run. His goal is to join us for a 5K run in April 2024.

He has moments when he tells me "I feel like myself again, my energy is back," and then he has moments when he feels so poor with no energy or stamina. He wants to retreat to the couch.

He finds the mornings are still a challenge. He is slow to get up and get going. His neuropathy is intermittent and some days the discomfort in his stomach makes it hard to eat. It's on these days he wonders if he'll ever fully recover from the chemo.

He is working full-time as a general medical doctor in a local hospital. He notices the demands of his job have made it challenging to focus on his health. This is one thing he wants to change, "I need to cut back, I'm so tired after seven days of work I have no energy to exercise."

We are in the process now of making these changes. This is not easy from a financial standpoint but also because his job is a big part of his identity. He is used to working and to cut back is going to be difficult.

What will he do with his spare time? How will our budget change month to month? These are questions he is wrestling with.

One thing we haven't done as a family since 2021 is travel. Jeff didn't feel he was ready. As we begin 2024 with negative tests and blood work, Jeff is considering travel. I am thrilled. This is a good sign. Perhaps, he is feeling more confident in his body and trusting he is truly in remission. We are now making plans to travel and go places.

We just took our first trip to Buffalo, New York in February 2024, during the kid's winter break. We had a wonderful time. We laughed a lot. We played cards. We gathered with friends around food. My husband shared stories that had us all in stitches.

It was a great week and one thing that made my life better— laughter with my husband and two children. The last two years were a strain on us all yet I'm grateful our family is stronger because of it. I'm thankful we didn't let cancer have power over our relationship. We stayed together. We are blessed we made it to the other side.

If you are walking this dark road, we pray our story gives you courage, hope, and a light. You are not alone.

It's Your Move:
Push-Up March
Check out the It's Your Move channel: www.youtube.com/@juliebhughes

EPILOGUE

I blink—
another year has gone.
Forty-four already?
My trouble—
I think I have more time.
Jack Kornfield nods as
he sits next to Mary Oliver.
They smile from across
the table. My notebook
ready…
She asks me the same
beautiful question from
last year—
"Tell me, what is it
you plan to do with your one
wild and precious life?"
Today—
I will…play outside,
pay attention and
rejoice in the Lord.

I was surrounded by trees, a clear sky, the waterway, and wildlife. I noticed how green the trail was—*wow look at all the cattails*— a red-winged blackbird must have heard me as it sang out. I spotted him hanging out on a cattail as I ran past.

Five miles in my right leg began to speak up. I took a deep breath. *What do I see?* A white butterfly then two, then three. Before I knew it, I was counting the white butterflies as I ran— my right leg discomfort softened.

I was at number 21 when a walker was heading my way. I couldn't wait to share with her all the butterflies out today and if she had noticed them too. I waved, smiled, "Good morning", and looked at her face as I slowed down to a jog.

She was looking down at her phone, earbuds in, eyes locked to the screen—I was hoping she would look up—but she didn't. She continued with no awareness of my presence. *Oh well*—I turned my attention to the water—*run on.*

To my surprise, I spotted two baby turtles swimming in the water. I stopped my watch and stood on the bank to get a closer look. One of the turtles swam up to the surface and poked its head out of the water. I was thrilled! It froze there looking at me as if to say—*I see you.*

I smiled. Creation had my back—birds, trees, butterflies, and turtles—they saw me. I saw them. Connection on the trail and why I kept coming back.

Grateful it was always available to me through this challenging year.

AFFIRMATIONS

Try on a few and see which ones resonate with you this week. Come back to this page as often as you wish. Write them down and place them in areas where you are most.

I'm beginning to believe I will have the strength to make it through.

I don't like what is happening but I have a choice of how I will show up for my family.

Through the use of a few simple tools, I will stay present in this moment

I am willing to ask for help

I am willing to find joy today

I am willing to learn to let myself be still

I am willing to have a teachable spirit

I am allowed to nurture myself

I am allowed to play and have fun

I am allowed to pivot and adapt

I am just here to love my spouse in this difficult circumstance

Being a caregiver is a blessing I accept

As I pray and listen, I will be led

I now accept hope.

I am safe and supported.

We will make it through this storm and come out the other side wiser, stronger, and kinder.

ACKNOWLEDGMENTS

I am deeply grateful to all who supported us during this difficult year and encouraged me as I wrote this book. There are so many folks who came alongside me and my family. Please know that even if I fail to mention you individually, you are cherished and I appreciate you.

Most importantly, thank you to my husband Jeff, and our children Brindsley and Delaney for allowing me to share our story. I hope it helps families, as I know you believe it will. I love you tremendously.

We are deeply grateful to Dr. Duffy, Dr. Granato, Taylor, Denise Lougee, and the healthcare team at Hematology Oncology Associates. Your exceptional kindness, compassion, and dedication guided us through Jeff's health challenge. Having access to world-class care locally was an invaluable gift. You have our sincerest thanks.

Thank you, Mom, for being available at a moment's notice to rearrange your schedule and help however needed. Your flexibility and can-do spirit uplifted us. We love you.

To my mother- and father-in-law Cathy and Dave Hughes - thank you for making long drives, taking Jeff to appointments, and helping with the kids. We are truly grateful. We love you.

Thank you, Dad, and Sally Dulcich-Bloom for your prayers and support. We love you.

Sincere gratitude to my siblings - Jon Bloom, Mandy Rundgren, Michelle Ball, and Becky Stanford - and their spouses Kristen, Shane, Chris, and Collin. Thank you for your prayers and support during this trial. We love you.

Profound gratitude to my sister-in-law Cindy and brother-in-law Dino Kotrides and family for your unwavering support and encouragement throughout this challenge. Thank you for providing meals and being available to both Jeff and me via phone and text - your frequent communication uplifted us more than you can imagine. We feel truly blessed to have you in our lives as both friends and family. We love you dearly.

And heartfelt appreciation to Aunt Colleen and Uncle Tim for taking Brindsley and Delaney on adventures and being early risers. We are forever grateful for your generosity and love.

Carrie-Anne Haag, Thank you for courageously walking alongside me as a true friend during this painful time. Your surprise visit, cards, gifts, snacks, songs, and laughs uplifted me and my family immensely. I feel so blessed to have your generous spirit in my life. Love you, buddy.

Felicia Case, Thank you for meeting me to run every Saturday, even when I was slow. Your companionship and encouragement kept me moving forward during the darkest days. I'm so grateful for our friendship and that you motivated me to continue running when I needed it most.

Stacey Sinclair, Your joyful spirit buoyed us during the storm. We're endlessly grateful for your generous support and encouragement.

Kharyn Tobin, Wise friend, thank you for the Bible verses that anchored me in grief. I'm grateful I could call on you in my darkest moments.

Carina Schoenberger, Your surprise meal and taking the kids to play were timely gifts. Your kindness will stay with us. Miss you, dear friend.

Katrina Gardner & Jaime Doolittle - It meant so much to Brindsley to have his friends running with him at The Good Samaritan Run. It uplifted us more than you know. You and your families are wonderful. Thank you.

Jenny & Dan Plewak - Your April visit and prayers were a blessing when we desperately needed uplifting. We're honored to know your family.

Thank you to my run coach and friend, Joel Sattgast. Even though I wasn't able to train with you, I'm grateful that you checked in on me and kept my family in your thoughts and prayers. It meant so much to know you were in our corner. Your friendship and support as my run coach have truly made a difference. Thank you for everything.

I want to thank The Run to Write Community on Substack. I'm so grateful for your generous support and uplifting words as I've shared excerpts from my book. In particular, I'd like to express my appreciation to community members Rebecca Holden, Amie McGraham, Gail Boenning, Clark Rose, Gary Spangler, Faith Hubbard, Nancy Dafoe, Claudette Henson, Mirtha Budow, Miriam Ilgenfritz, Jack McNulty, Melissa Timko, Donna Rice, Holly Rabalais, and Sharon Shimpach. Your kindness, encouragement, and love for our community have meant the world to me.

I extend my deepest gratitude to the Writing In Community (WIC) Alumni: Terri Tomoff, Janis Farmer, Michal Berman, Heather Button, Russell John, Diane Osgood, Kathy Karn, Julie Rains, Wendy Coad, Kym Dakin, Cindy Villanueva, Linda Platt, Frauke, Linda McLachlan, Bill Tomoff, Annette Mason, Katy Dalgleish, Salman Ansari, Jackie Alcalde Marr, Joann Malone, Margaret O'Brien, and Kathy Taylor. Your warmth and positivity truly uplifted me. I also want to thank the Purple Space community friends - Louise Karch, Annie Parnell, Heat Dziczek, Júlio Baptista Barroco, Darin Simmons, Inbar Lee Hyams, Jessica Zou, Amanda Hsiung-Blodgett, Pegret Harrison, Khushi Katyal, Tonya Cole, and Olabanji Stephen. Thank you for making it a welcoming place to share vulnerably.

Pastor Kim, thank you for coming each week to pray and talk with Jeff. I'm so happy I called you for help and thank you for answering me with such love, compassion, and kindness. We are so grateful our paths crossed and you were here for our family. I hope you know how much we appreciate you.

Thank you to our community of family and friends who sent meals, gift cards, letters, uplifting messages, helped with yard work, and kept us in prayer— Aunt Lorrie, Aunt Linda, Gram, Denise Bertholf, Andrea Munsee, Bethany Fassler, Abby Morton, Keri Stevens, Cassi Crossman, Debi Rotondo, Linda Pelland, Jeanne Cioci, Leigh Strait, Liz Wicher, Melissa Mapstone, Karen Grimshaw, Faith Hubbard, Luke Lawyer, and Sarah & Jim Starwotiz for the amazing beanie hats with beards for Jeff. Church members of the United Methodist Church of Manlius— Claudette Henson, Linny Hernandez, Diana Bishop Cordes, Bruce Cordes, Sunny Kim, Sophia Suri, Karen Burns, Patrick and Sandra O'Connor and so many others. You are a blessing.

Most of all, thank you, God, for carrying us through this darkness. Thank you for healing Jeff, and protecting my family. We felt Your light and hope every step of the way. Your grace, mercy, and love sustained us. Thank you for all the ways you bless us and may we lean on you always.

RESOURCES

Testicular Awareness Foundation:
https://www.testicularcancerawarenessfoundation.org/

Nuts & Bolts Website: https://nutsandbolts.movember.com/

Website: Manuptocancer.com

Facebook Group: Man Up to Cancer

Testicular Cancer Society: https://testicularcancersociety.org/

ABOUT THE AUTHOR

Julie B. Hughes is a mother, writer, marathoner, and physical therapist. She leads The Run to Write Club to unite movement and writing through an encouraging community. Both pursuits require courage; together we can take one step and one word at a time.

She lives in Central New York with her husband and two children. She believes life's challenges help us grow and discover our capabilities. Her books and poetry aim to inspire readers to "lean into their stories of challenge with curiosity and courage."

How To Stay In Touch:

Website: www.juliebhughes.com

It's Your Move Channel: https://youtube.com/@juliebhughes

Join the Run to Write Community: https://juliebhughes.substack.com

Other Books by Julie B. Hughes

My Road: A Runner's Journey Through Persistent Pain to Healing, 2021

Running Into Poetry: An invitation to be present on your path, 2022

Staring Down a Dream: A Mom, a Marathoner, a Mission, 2023

Please rate A REAL BALLBUSTER:
Untangling Testicular Cancer Together

What resonated with you? What moved you or jumped out at you?

The next time you're on Amazon, please give it a couple of words and as many stars as you like. The biggest challenge for an author is promotion, and what people see on Amazon makes a big difference. It means everything to me as a self-publisher.

Thank you so much for your support.

Take good care,

Julie B.

Made in the USA
Middletown, DE
05 April 2024

52433378R00109